*Touring
the
Coastal
Georgia
Backroads*

ALSO BY NANCY RHYNE

Touring the Coastal South Carolina Backroads
The Grand Strand: An Uncommon Guide to Myrtle Beach and Its Surroundings
Carolina Seashells
Tales of the South Carolina Low Country
More Tales of the South Carolina Low Country
Coastal Ghosts: Haunted Places from Wilmington to Savannah
Murder in the Carolinas
Once Upon a Time on a Plantation
Plantation Tales
More Murder in the Carolinas
Alice Flagg: The Ghost of the Hermitage
The South Carolina Lizard Man

OTHER TITLES IN JOHN F. BLAIR'S *TOURING THE BACKROADS* SERIES

Touring the Western North Carolina Backroads by Carolyn Sakowski
Touring the East Tennessee Backroads by Carolyn Sakowski
Touring the Coastal South Carolina Backroads by Nancy Rhyne

Touring the Coastal Georgia Backroads

Nancy Rhyne

JOHN F. BLAIR
PUBLISHER
WINSTON-SALEM,
NORTH CAROLINA

BOOK DESIGN BY DEBRA LONG HAMPTON
PRINTED AND BOUND BY R. R. DONNELLEY & SONS

*The paper in this book meets the guidelines
for permanence and durability of the
Committee on Production Guidelines for Book Longevity
of the Council on Library Resources.*

Photographs on front cover, clockwise from top left—

Marine Center from The Wormsloe Tour
Tybee Lighthouse from The Tybee Light Tour
The Pink House from The Lincoln's Christmas Gift Tour
Savannah Cotton Exchange from The Old Seaport Tour
The Jekyll Island Club from The Marshes of Glynn Tour
Fountain in Forsyth Park from The Lincoln's Christmas Gift Tour

Library of Congress Cataloging-in-Publication Data

Rhyne, Nancy, 1926–
Touring the coastal Georgia backroads / Nancy Rhyne.
    p.   cm.
Includes bibliographical references (p.   ) and index.
ISBN 0-89587-111-4
1. Georgia—Tours.   2. Automobile travel—Georgia—Guidebooks.
I. Title.
F284.3.R48   1994
917.58'70443—dc20   93–47130

To

Margaret Clayton,
well-loved patron
of Charlotte-area writers

Table of Contents

Preface

I wrote this book because I had to.

As I was working on *Touring the Coastal South Carolina Backroads*, many people commented to me on Georgia's coast. "You'll have to remember that South Carolina was founded by aristocrats, while Georgia was founded by crooks," someone said, a misrepresentation if there ever was one. "If you like South Carolina's barrier islands, you should visit Georgia's Golden Isles," someone else said. And when I missed church for several Sundays while researching this book, my minister remarked, "You must have covered Georgia about as well as Sherman." Everybody, it seemed, had an opinion about coastal Georgia. I felt compelled to find out about the area firsthand.

I was not disappointed.

At historic Midway Church, I discovered a man in overalls scrubbing the floor who knew more of Georgia's history than many a Ph.D. In Claxton, I heard about the best down-home, foot-stomping rattlesnake roundup this side of Texas. In Savannah, I visited the square where local character Sheftall Sheftall greeted the Marquis de Lafayette in 1825. In the Okefenokee Swamp, I rode a boat through black water thick with alligators. In Brunswick, I learned about a World War II "Blimp Base" that helped defeat the Nazis. On Cockspur Island, I discovered why John Wesley, the founder of the Methodist church, left Georgia in such a hurry. I even managed to track down the elusive Button Gwinnett, who once owned St. Catherines Island.

And that was only the beginning.

The first settlers of Georgia were 35 carefully selected English families. These were soon followed by a company of Austrian Lutherans from Salzburg seeking asylum from Catholic persecution. They settled at Ebenezer in what is now Effingham County. Then, as a barrier against the Spanish at St. Augustine, Florida, James Oglethorpe induced some Scottish Highlanders of the McIntosh clan to come over. These 160 men and 50 women and children settled at New Inverness, now Darien, at the mouth of the Altamaha River. Then came more English and Germans, a sprinkling of Huguenots, some Spanish and Portuguese Jews, and a few Scotch and Scotch-Irish.

It was a cosmopolitan little colony, but not a prosperous one. At the end of the proprietary period, there were fewer than 2,500 people in the whole province. With the establishment of the royal government in 1753, conditions started to improve. Immigrants began settling near the coast and along the rivers.

There followed wars and peace, depressions and recoveries. Before the turn of this century, millionaires from the North discovered the Golden Isles and built the Jekyll Island Club. Clubs were constructed on other islands as well, and no longer was Georgia spoken of merely as the state over which Sherman marched on his way to the sea.

Today, coastal Georgia is a prime destination for visitors from all over the map. But those visitors will be selling the area short unless they are willing to explore the backroads, to acquaint themselves with coastal Georgia's rich history—to seek out the forts erected on almost every bluff as deterrents to the Spanish, perhaps, or to ask why St. Patrick's Day is such a major event in Savannah.

The tours in this book range from the rural to the urban—from the well-traveled squares of Savannah to the sparsely populated spaces around the Okefenokee Swamp. You may want to combine some of the shorter tours or divide some of the longer ones.

Of course, the streets in Savannah's historic district and the road around the perimeter of Jekyll Island hardly qualify as backroads. Yet it seemed unfair to write a book about coastal Georgia and neglect places so rich in history. Even in the case of popular tourist spots, I have tried to uncover interesting, unusual, or little-known tidbits of local history. I hope that effort has been a success.

This is not meant to be a comprehensive guide to all the worthwhile sites on Georgia's coast. There is no way I could take readers down every out-of-the-way lane that offers an interesting story. It is my hope that you will pursue roads outside the bounds of these tours whenever the mood strikes, that you will seek out those places and stories in coastal Georgia that have special meaning for you.

Acknowledgments

On the day before Thanksgiving 1992, I called Katy McDonough in the Manuscripts Division at the Library of Congress and explained that I was writing a book on coastal Georgia. I wanted to know what manuscripts in the collection gave accounts of the people who had lived on the coast. During the 1930s, writers employed by the Works Progress Administration had visited country people in coastal Georgia and elsewhere to record their reminiscences. Katy assured me that the collection held a large volume of personal stories. She advised me how to get my hands on those tales, and I thank her for her substantial contribution to this book.

In the fall of 1992, as I sat in the lobby of Georgia State University autographing books at the Atlanta International Reading Festival, in walked Faith Brunson, formerly the book buyer for Rich's Department Stores, and now the organizer of Rich's book signings. We immediately became friends. I couldn't get enough of Faith's knowledge of books and authors. Since that day, she has helped me in many ways, including setting up appointments with people to be interviewed and giving me information on coastal Georgia.

Others whom I thank for their cheerful help include the staff at the University of Georgia Press; the Newport (Rhode Island) Historical Society staff; Mary Lou Waters with the Georgia Department of Natural Resources; Carl E. Gravlin, the custodian of the Georgia Salzburger Museum in Rincon;

Sidney L. Waldhour, Jr., of Rincon; Bobbie I. Dugger of Savannah; Barry Stokes and Sharon Wixom of Chatham-Effingham-Liberty Regional Library in Savannah; Eileen Ielmini of the Georgia Historical Society in Savannah; Barbara Heuer, formerly of the Georgia Historical Society; Rebecca Novy of the Girl Scout Council of Savannah; Janet Carol Waters, director of Davenport House Museum in Savannah; Maurice M. "Chuck" Witherspoon, the town crier of the Historic Savannah Foundation; Michael Jacobs of Wormsloe State Historic Site; Linda King of the Coastal Georgia Historical Society on St. Simons Island; Minnie Johnson at Blue Goose Country Collectibles in St. Marys; and Mary Graham of Charlotte, North Carolina.

There aren't words to describe how I feel about the people at John F. Blair, Publisher. The help given me by Lisa Wagoner, Carolyn Sakowski, and Steve Kirk overwhelms me. This project took weeks and weeks of their time. Now that Carolyn is president of the company, she still gives me her time generously. They are the people who have made my dreams come true.

Thanks to Sid for the photos and help during the hot summer of 1993. I couldn't ask for a better "better half."

*Touring
the
Coastal
Georgia
Backroads*

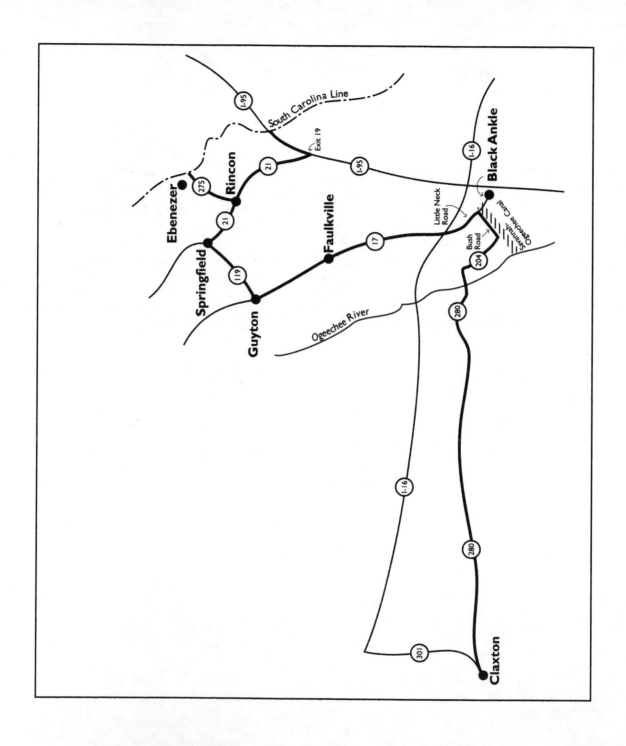

The Salzburger Tour

This tour starts in Ebenezer, heads to Springfield and Guyton, and visits the Black Ankle section of Chatham County. It then follows the Savannah-Ogeechee Canal before ending in Claxton.

Total mileage: approximately 84 miles.

To reach the historic site of Ebenezer (sometimes called New Ebenezer), take Exit 19 off I-95; this is the first exit beyond the Georgia Welcome Center, just south of the South Carolina border. Head west on GA 21 for 11.3 miles through the small town of Rincon to GA 275, also known as Ebenezer Road. Turn right on GA 275 and travel 5.4 miles through a wooded area to Ebenezer.

A colony of Lutherans from Salzburg, Austria, arrived in Savannah on March 12, 1734. The Salzburgers, as they were known, were seeking freedom of worship. Led by John Martin Bolzius (sometimes spelled Boltius), an industrious minister who taught himself English on the voyage across the Atlantic so he would be able to communicate with the officials in Georgia, and Israel Christian Gronau, the Salzburgers were directed about 35 miles up the Savannah River by General James Oglethorpe. It was there, on a tract of land on Ebenezer Creek about 6 miles from the river, that they established the community of Ebenezer.

After two years of sickness and struggle, they realized that this location would never become a permanent home. In 1736, they moved the 6 miles to the banks of the Savannah River and established a new settlement. Laid out by Noble Jones in a manner similar to Savannah, this community retained the name of Ebenezer.

The Salzburgers prospered in their new setting. It was said that the most economical housewives and the most frugal husbands in all of Georgia were to be found here.

The residents discovered a profitable source of income in the production of silk. The silk culture was introduced to Ebenezer in 1736, when each Salzburger family was given a white mulberry tree from Trustees' Garden in Savannah. (For more information about Trustees' Garden, see The Old Seaport Tour, page 45.)

The process of making silk is an interesting one. When silkworms are full-grown, they are ready to spin their cocoons. Once the worms begin to look for twigs on which to fasten their cocoons, the silk farmer places each inside a tiny cell within a larger rack of such cells. As the worm begins to spin its cocoon, a gluelike fluid comes out of its upper lip. When the fluid hits the air, it hardens into fine silk thread. The worm spins the outer covering of its cocoon and then winds the long thread of silk around its body. Before the insect can emerge, the cocoon is placed in boiling water. Then the farmer begins to unwind the threads. The ends of four or five cocoons are twisted together and put into a guide much like the eye of a needle. The silk is wound around a reel; sometimes, a single silk thread can reach a length of 1,000 feet. Each thread is so fine that it would take about 1,000 miles of it to make a pound of raw silk.

John Martin Bolzius's wife eventually became the leader of the silk culture in Ebenezer. By 1749, the community produced 762 pounds of cocoons, which yielded 50 pounds of raw silk. From these 50 pounds, 13 ounces of spun silk were produced.

Although the silk culture declined throughout the rest of Georgia, the Salzburgers persevered. In 1772, they shipped 485 pounds of raw silk. Their silk began to earn a reputation for its high quality. Some years, they produced over 2,000 pounds of silk for export to England. The sale of silk proved such a good source of income for the villagers that Ebenezer became known as the "Silk Capital."

The Revolutionary War brought bad times to the area. The British used Ebenezer as a holding center for prisoners. Homes were burned, possessions stolen, and gardens ruined. Many citizens abandoned the town. The British also set up drink houses, and some of the Salzburgers, formerly a very sober people, began to imbibe as well. Those citizens who returned after the war were discouraged by the ruin they found. By 1850, there were only two houses left in town.

Arriving in Ebenezer today, one of the first things you will see is Jerusalem Lutheran Church. This is actually the second such church. The first was built near the site of the present church in 1741. The first church constructed in Georgia, it served as a place of worship until the present brick structure was completed.

The present church is the oldest building in Georgia. Construction began in 1767 and was completed in 1769. The bricks were made from local clay and were probably fired over open flames. Women and children carried the bricks from the kiln to the church site. Some of the bricks bear the fingerprints of the

Salzburger Cabin

children who carried them; these can be seen on the front of the building today. The church walls are twenty inches thick. The lumber was sawed at a sawmill built by the Salzburgers in 1757. The bells in the belfry are the oldest in Georgia. You can even see the date 1769 chiseled in a brick at the peak of the church, over the clock.

During the Revolutionary War, the church was used first as a hospital, then as a storehouse, and finally as a horse stable. The bleached spots on the exterior came about when salt was stored against the wall.

Near the church is the Salzburger Museum, built on the site of the first orphanage in Georgia. The two-story brick building houses artifacts from the early days of the settlement. Here, you can see a Bible brought by the first Salzburgers when they arrived in Georgia, along with other relics such as a crystal punch bowl and cups, a pump organ, farm implements, Civil War weapons, and a Civil War mending kit, which includes needles, pins, thread, and a sheet of Confederate money. Upstairs, you can see replicas of the old looms that were used during the days of silk production. One of the most interesting items in the museum is a turkey bell. This bell was borne by one turkey in the flock. The tinkling bell provided evidence of the flock's whereabouts.

It is even rumored that the museum has a ghost. The caretaker's dogs have

Salzburger Cemetery

been known to bark at something on the stairs when nothing is visible to the human eye.

At the edge of the community, across from the church and the museum, is the cemetery. Many of the grave markers are made of wood, and the names of the deceased and their dates of birth and death have long since disappeared. The cemetery contains a monument to John Martin Bolzius and Israel Christian Gronau, the ministers who led the first Salzburgers. The actual burial sites of Bolzius and Gronau have never been determined, though some believe they are in a cemetery south of Ebenezer.

The heritage of the original Ebenezer settlers is still strongly preserved today. For many years, descendants of the Salzburgers have gathered on March 12, the anniversary of the arrival of their ancestors in America.

This event became so popular that in 1929, the group began holding Labor Day picnics as well. Each year on Labor Day, the open, grassy lawn surrounding Jerusalem Lutheran Church becomes the scene of a big family reunion when the members of the Salzburger Society gather. This celebration begins with a religious service and is a time of remembering the pioneers, telling stories, and swapping recipes. The officers of the society speak on the history of the group, lauding eminent citizens who have descended from their ranks and relating future plans for the organization.

Some of the elderly members of the society remember the days when real German recipes added zest to the Salzburgers' old picnic gatherings. During the late 1930s, reporters from the Works Progress Administration interviewed attendees at one of these meetings. An eminent judge who was a direct descendant of one of the original Salzburgers offered a description of picnics he remembered from his youth:

> Just ordinary pigs never went into the making of that sausage meat. Corn-fed hogs, the very best, were used and a finer pork you've never tasted. The hogs had to be fattened at least two years on corn before they were considered fit. Wines made from Austrian recipes made the old picnickers merry in former days, but the present custom is to serve nothing stronger than coffee. Year by year all the old German foods have been replaced by Southern American cooking. Even sour potato salad and Austrian jellies have disappeared.

Material collected by the Georgia Writers' Project in the 1930s offers some interesting recipes that were served at Salzburger gatherings. One favorite was "mulatto rice," which received its name because of its yellow-red color. The interviewer recorded this description of its preparation: "It's easy to make. You just throw some bacon in a pot and fry it brown, then you throw in a couple of cans of tomatoes and some onions and cayenne pepper and salt, a little parsley, and maybe a little garlic. Throw in a couple of pounds of washed rice and let it all steam for an hour."

In former days, the yearly festival ended with the descendants singing the old Salzburger Exile Song:

I am a wretched exile here—
Thus must my name be given—
From Native land and all's that dear,
For God's word, I am driven.

Full well I know, Lord Jesus Christ,
Thy treatment was no better;
Thy follower I now will be;
To do thy will I'm debtor.

Henceforth, a pilgrim I must be,
In foreign climes must wander;
Oh Lord! My prayer ascends to thee,
That thou my path will ponder.

My God conduct me to a place
Though in some distant nation,
Where I may have thy glorious word,
And learn thy great Salvation.

Today, part of the town of Ebenezer is being rebuilt as the New Ebenezer Retreat Center. The main building can sleep forty-eight and accommodate three hundred for meetings and meals. Placed on lots where original cottages once stood, the eight new cottages at the retreat center look like their long-ago predecessors on the outside but have all the creature comforts inside. The retreat center is designed for the use of Christians of all denominations, and for families as well.

After viewing Ebenezer, backtrack on GA 275 to Rincon and turn right on GA 21. Continue 3 miles through the rolling countryside for a quick trip to Springfield. The town's name was taken from a mineral spring discovered in a field by early settlers. The Effingham County seat was changed five times before finally being established here in 1832. It is 1.5 miles from the town limits to a sign directing you to the Effingham County Courthouse. Turn right and proceed one block to Rabon Street. This courthouse, designed by Savannah architect Hyman W. Witcover, was built in 1908. It features a Jeffersonian dome and a classical Greek portico. The classical Greek style was frequently used for courthouses around the turn of the century.

Once you have seen the courthouse, begin retracing your route. After 0.2 mile, turn right on GA 119. It is 5 miles to the Guyton city limits.

Guyton was developed in 1838 as a railroad town and a summer resort for Savannah residents. During the heyday of the railroads, as many as eight passenger trains served Guyton every day. During the Civil War, the railroads were used to transport wounded soldiers to the Confederate General Hospital in Guyton. General William T. Sherman's men destroyed the railroad as they traveled through Effingham County on their "March to the Sea." About ten years after the war, Guyton experienced an influx of new residents, as people from Savannah fled their city to escape a yellow fever epidemic.

Today, it seems that every street in this small town has historic homes in a wealth of architectural styles, including Greek Revival, Italianate, and Queen Anne. A tour of some of Guyton's historic homes is a popular event every Christmas season.

It is 0.1 mile from the city limits to Magnolia Street. Turn right. After 0.7 mile

Effingham County Courthouse

TOURING THE COASTAL GEORGIA BACKROADS

on Magnolia, turn right on Alexander Street. New Hope A.M.E. Church is the last building on the left in the first block. Constructed in 1885, this simple, elegant frame church is one of the oldest and best preserved in Georgia. Its projecting entrance and belfry are typical of Southern church construction of the late nineteenth century. Situated in the historically black neighborhood of Sugar Hill, New Hope A.M.E. Church is listed on the National Register of Historic Places.

Claudette's Country Kitchen and Inn

Backtrack to GA 119 (Springfield Avenue) and turn right. After 0.3 mile, turn right on Central Boulevard (GA 17).

The home at 106 Central Boulevard is the red-roofed Davant-Thompson-Rahn House, built around 1868. Herman Hirsch, the quartermaster in charge of Confederate hospitals, constructed this house for the Davant family. During the yellow fever epidemic of 1876, William and Nellie Gordon of Savannah came with their family to take refuge with the Davants. While staying here, Nellie Gordon wrote a letter describing how she had witnessed the deaths of some forty-five yellow fever victims in just one day. The letter was penned in a style called "cross writing," used mainly because of the shortage of paper and the expense of postage. Escaping the epidemic with her parents in Guyton was young Juliette Gordon, the future founder of the Girl Scouts. (For more information on Juliette Gordon Low, see The Lincoln's Christmas Gift Tour, pages 25–26.)

108 Central Boulevard

Today, the Davant-Thompson-Rahn House is more popularly known as Claudette's Country Kitchen and Inn. Patrons agree that to savor a meal in the dining room here is to enjoy the best of Old South cooking. Suites are available for overnight guests.

The house next door at 108 Central Boulevard, another white clapboard building with a red roof, is especially pleasing during the Christmas season, when it is lavishly decorated.

Continue through a small business district to see the Cubbedge House, located at 506 Central Boulevard; built around 1892, this beautiful home is surrounded by a well-kept lawn and a picket fence.

The Cubbedge House

These few homes are only a sample of what historic Guyton has to offer. If you have the time, you cannot go wrong by meandering the side streets of this lovely town.

After 0.5 mile on Central Boulevard, turn left on Cemetery Road. After one block, turn left on West Central Boulevard. The railroad tracks, once the hub of activity in Guyton, ran down what is now the wide, grassy median between Central Boulevard and West Central Boulevard.

It is 0.5 mile to GA 119 (Springfield Avenue). Turn left. After one block, turn right on Central Boulevard (GA 17) and head out of Guyton.

Drive 13.4 miles to the village of Faulkville. Continue another 5.4 miles on GA 17 to where it ends at the intersection with U.S. 16. Head directly across U.S. 16 and continue straight; though there is no sign at the intersection, you are now on Little Neck Road. It is 4.7 miles to Bethel Baptist Church, which is part of the community once known as Black Ankle. The church is on the right and its cemetery on the left.

Black Ankle first attracted outside attention around 1920. Although near the great seaport of Savannah, it was located on an isolated strip on the northwest border of Chatham County. On one side, it was hemmed in by the broad waters of the Ogeechee River. On the other three sides, it was cut off from civilization by heavily wooded marsh and tracts of pine forest through which there were no passable roads for many years.

House at Black Ankle

Strangers gave the area its name because the feet of the local inhabitants were often coated with black ooze from traveling barefoot through the mud.

At the time of their "discovery," Black Ankle residents, of English descent, lived by their own set of laws. They had little desire to associate with people outside their community. Fishing parties from Savannah began to return with tales of wild men who took shots at them from behind trees along a certain section of the Ogeechee River. People began to believe it was dangerous for a stranger to venture into this unknown territory. Communities on the fringe of Black Ankle reported that a strange, hostile tribe of white people lived there, that members of the group rarely emerged from their isolation, and that the colony was apparently bent on retaining its seclusion.

One story was told of a hunter who was lost for several hours in the junglelike labyrinth of the Black Ankle forest. He heard the cracking of twigs and the rustling of leaves, as if somebody were following him through the woods. When he finally found his way back to civilization, he reported that he had heard whispering or hissing on several occasions but had never seen a human soul.

The area was finally opened to civilization when government workers offering social services found their way into Black Ankle in the late 1930s. Traveling in an automobile, armed with pistols, agents pushed inward along an old, broken, weedy path that showed little evidence of recent use. They crossed two ditches bridged with ancient logs before stumbling upon Black Ankle.

They discovered a community that had changed little in over a century. The people lived in one-room log huts like those built by early English settlers. Cooking utensils were nonexistent, except for frying pans and one-gallon tin cans. Electricity and gas were unknown. The residents presented a hostile front. Women and children scurried out of sight into their huts. Men stood close-mouthed and suspicious, fingers ready on the triggers of their sawed-off shotguns.

Until World War II, the people of Black Ankle looked with hostility on all outsiders except well-known county workers. That distrust served to keep their ancestral customs intact. Because the idea of receiving letters was unknown to them, local residents refused to affix their marks to papers endorsing a rural mail route. Even medical assistance was not always accepted. Even today, many of the residents remain hesitant about talking to strangers.

One current resident related several interesting details about life in the early Black Ankle settlement. "Back then," he explained, "everybody lived out of the woods, garden, and river, and they growed what they ate. A flock of fifty wild turkeys were close to my house. They were small, but they were good." This same gentleman revealed that he had once worked for the Central of Georgia Railroad. "I worked hard and would have made engineer," he said, "except I couldn't write and was unable to fill out the forms."

He went on to say that even as close-knit as the area's residents appear to outsiders, they still have their feuds. "My great-uncle and ol' man Clanton got into it over some property lines," he explained. "They went down in the swamp and got in a dispute as to just where the property line was. You know, it's hard to tell where a property line is in a swamp. Ol' man Clanton got so mad at my great-uncle that he shot his hat off." As he pointed across the road, the speaker said, "They are both over there in Bethel Cemetery now, and they didn't take an acre of land with them."

Today, there is little left of this isolated community. A brick structure has replaced the original wooden Bethel Baptist Church. Bethel School, which once stood next to the church, is no longer in existence. But Bethel Cemetery can still be seen in its lovely setting. Graves are spread under moss-draped oak trees. The inscription on the marker for Jacob Gould indicates that he lived from 1778 to 1868 and donated the land for the cemetery. The man who shared his memories of early Black Ankle noted that his mother and his father's mother were both Goulds. He was proud of the fact that his father lacked only two months of being ninety-nine when he died.

Bethel Cemetery

Backtrack 0.3 mile on Little Neck Road and turn left on Bush Road. As you

drive Bush Road, you are actually traveling on what was formerly part of the historic Savannah-Ogeechee Canal. The portion now used as a roadbed has been filled in. The other half of the canal, located immediately to your right, remains picturesque. You can still see the old brick locks that were used to raise and lower the water level.

Built from 1828 to 1831, this 17.5-mile canal stretched from the Ogeechee River to the Savannah River. Much like the Erie Canal, it utilized horses to pull flat-bottomed barges. Those barges carried rice, lumber, bricks, and farm produce to and from Savannah. The canal had four lift locks and two tidal locks. It remained active until the 1860s, when railroad construction made canals obsolete.

During the Civil War, the canal was the location of a skirmish on December 6, 1864, when Sherman forced Southern defenders to cross the canal and withdraw toward Savannah during his famous "March to the Sea."

After the Civil War, the canal lay in a state of disrepair until 1982, when local people proposed a major cleanup project. In recent years, efforts have been made to turn the canal and its right of way into a recreational facility for canoeing, boating, jogging, and other recreational activities.

It is 2.6 miles to where Bush Road ends at GA 204; the canal continues straight ahead. Turn right on GA 204. Travel 17.1 miles through sand hills covered in scrub pines, farms, and wooded tracts to U.S. 280. Turn left and

Savannah-Ogeechee Canal

head west for 4.8 miles to Pembroke. Continue 12.8 miles to Daisy, a shady village where lovely homes sit in groves of trees and large, immaculate lawns testify to careful upkeep. The lawns are shaded by pecan, pine, and oak trees.

Continue on U.S. 280 for 3.6 miles to the town of Claxton, which was established around 1894. The 1900 census recorded a population of fewer than three hundred, but by 1910, the town had more than six hundred people. It was named for a popular actress of the time, Kate Claxton.

Turn left onto South Claxton Avenue and drive until you reach a warehouse marked "Claxton Warehouse, Inc., Tobacco, Tomato Plants, Grain." This is the site of the annual Rattlesnake Roundup, one of the events for which Claxton is famous.

On the second weekend in March, this warehouse turns into a festive place featuring music, arts and crafts, beauty contests, and, of course, rattlesnakes. The rattlesnakes are packed into the back of the building. Although they are all Eastern diamondbacks, these snakes come in all sizes and shapes: long, thin ones; short, fat ones; and some ten- or twelve-pounders that stretch more than six feet. Visitors can purchase the skin, venom, and meat of snakes at the warehouse.

Mike Farrow of the Evans County Wildlife Club explained how the snakes are captured: "We take a long plastic pipe which we stick down in the burrow holes. We listen through the end of the pipe for the sound of rattles. The pipes are so sensitive that we can even hear mosquitoes buzzing around. After we find a rattlesnake, we dig it out with a shovel. There are a lot of holes that have snakes, but if we don't hear the rattles we don't know they are in there. Sometimes, we find two or three in a hole.

The "milker"

"Another way we can find the snakes is to hunt in warm weather. The warmer the weather, the closer to the mouth of the hole the snake comes. We take a mirror and reflect the light down in the hole. Sometimes, they are lying about two feet down in the hole. We use a hook and drag them out and don't have to go to the trouble of digging them out. When it gets even warmer, the snake will crawl out and lie beside the hole. We have to be careful. Sometimes, two or three are lying around near the hole. You could step on one.

"We advise nobody to handle snakes. We do not touch the snakes at all. That is left up to the specialists. We have one man who milks snakes."

"Milking" is the process used to remove venom from a snake's fangs. The snake is lifted out of the cage with a hook. The milker proceeds to a table with a container on it. For an instant, the milker stares at the snake, contemplating the exact time to grab it from behind the head. He then grabs the head and

---

presses the snake's jaws in such a way that the mouth is opened. The snake's fangs are then hooked onto the top of the container. As the milker squeezes the snake's jaws, the venom comes out of the mouth into the can. If you attend the Rattlesnake Roundup, you can see a live demonstration of this procedure.

In 1992, 433 snakes were captured for the roundup. Hunters turned in only 386 in 1993, and gusty winds, snow flurries, and bone-chilling temperatures kept the crowd to fewer than five thousand spectators. However, on more temperate weekends, the event usually draws more than twenty-five thousand visitors to the area.

Retrace your route to U.S. 280 (East Main Street) and turn left. Continue through the business district to Grady Street, where you will see a large brick building on the right bearing a sign reading "Claxton Fruit Cake, Claxton Bakery."

Claxton has always been an agricultural community. Through the years, area farms have produced poultry, cattle, hogs, goats, cotton, tobacco, fruit, honey, and timber. But Claxton's greatest claim to fame is its reputation as the "Fruitcake Capital of the World."

In 1927, eleven-year-old Albert Parker was hired as a floor sweeper in a Claxton bakery owned by an Italian immigrant named Savino Tos. Eighteen years later, Parker purchased the bakery. An astute businessman, he decided

Claxton Fruit Cake building

TOURING THE COASTAL GEORGIA BACKROADS

to actively market the bakery's fruitcakes. In 1952, a businessman who was active in the Civitan International organization decided to sell the Claxton fruitcakes as a fund-raising project in his Tampa, Florida, chapter. The project was so successful that the sale of fruitcakes became a national Civitan project, and Parker had to expand his facility. Today, the factory churns out 6,000,000 pounds of fruitcake a year. That's 900 miles of one-pound cakes placed end to end.

The process begins in the batter room, where workers mix eggs, flour, and other ingredients into batter. Buckets holding 70 pounds of batter are rolled into the next room, where cartons of cherries, pineapples, raisins, orange and lemon peel, pecans, walnuts, and almonds are dumped in. The batch, by now weighing 375 pounds, is stirred with a mixer so large it brings to mind a cement mixer. The next step is pouring the batter into pans and moving it by conveyor belt into the seven massive ovens that bake 86,000 pounds of cake daily at 350 degrees. After an hour and forty-five minutes of baking, the hot fruitcakes are taken into cooling rooms, where they sit for six hours at forty-five degrees. After cooling, the cakes are cut into one-pound loaves and individually wrapped and boxed.

Today, Claxton Bakery is still owned by the Parker family. The fruitcakes are still sold primarily by the twelve hundred Civitan clubs in the country. Ironically, Claxton does not have its own Civitan club.

Although health regulations prohibit tours of the Claxton Bakery, you can still buy fruitcakes at the bakery shop, which is open Monday through Saturday.

After you've had your fill of fruitcake and rattlesnakes, you can return to I-95 by retracing U.S. 280 and GA 204 or taking U.S. 301 north to I-16 which travels east to I-95.

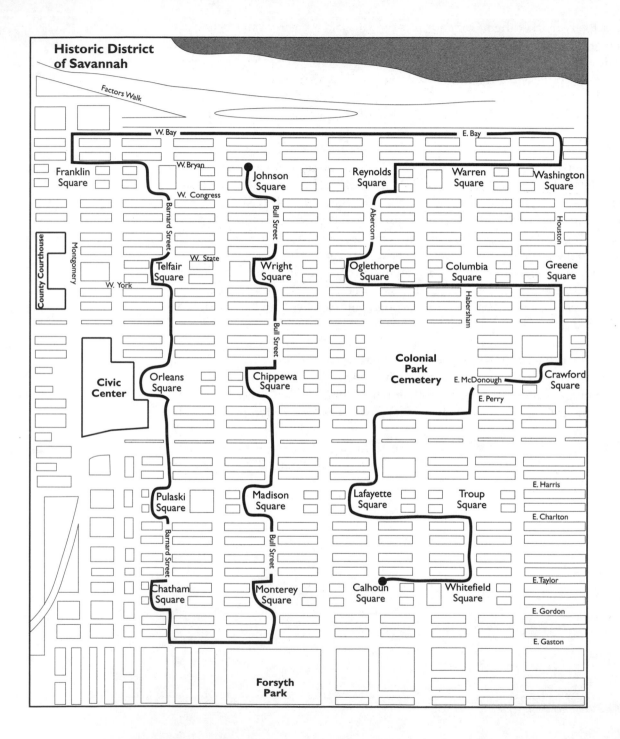

The Lincoln's Christmas Gift Tour

This tour covers the various squares in downtown Savannah—Johnson, Wright, Chippewa, Madison, Monterey, Chatham, Pulaski, Orleans, Telfair, Franklin, Washington, Warren, Reynolds, Oglethorpe, Columbia, Greene, Crawford, Lafayette, Troup, Whitefield, and Calhoun. It also includes Forsyth Park and Colonial Park Cemetery.

Total mileage: approximately 5 miles.

One of the best ways to explore Savannah's history is to tour the squares of its downtown area. In 1736, Francis Moore, a visitor to Savannah, wrote this description of the city:

> The town is laid out for two hundred and forty freeholds; the quantity of land necessary for that number is twenty-four square miles; every forty houses in town make a ward, to which four square miles in the country belong; each ward has a constable, and under him four tithing men. Where the town land ends, the villages begin; four villages make a ward out, which depends upon one of the wards within the town. The use of this is, in case a war should happen, the villages without may have places in the town to bring their cattle and families into for refuge, and for that purpose there is a square left in every ward, big enough for the outwards to camp in.

The original city plan still exists, with twenty of the twenty-four squares intact today.

This tour begins at Johnson Square, the oldest square in the city, located on Bull Street. The square is two blocks from Bay Street, which parallels the Savannah River one block from the waterfront. For the purposes of this tour, you may require the use of a car to explore all the squares in one day. However, it is highly recommended that you take every opportunity to get out and stroll through the squares to savor the history and beauty of the city. The best way to see Savannah's squares in undoubtedly on foot.

In 1732, King George II of England granted a charter to a group of trustees to establish the colony of Georgia in America. Spain, which had already claimed the same territory, protested to England, but the protest was ignored.

There were three principal motives behind the settlement effort. The first was philanthropic: victims of England's oppressive debt laws were to be given an opportunity to "escape" debtor's prison by becoming colonists. The second was economic: it was believed that Georgia could produce silk and wine, which England was buying at great expense from other nations. The third was military: Georgia would serve as a buffer for the established colony of South Carolina, which had previously undergone attack by Spaniards based in Florida. Over time, this third motive became the most important.

General James Edward Oglethorpe, a member of Parliament, was the guiding force behind the colony. When he undertook the leadership position, he was in the prime of life—tall, handsome, the *beau idéal* of an English gentleman. He volunteered to accompany the colonists to the New World.

In 1732, Oglethorpe and 114 colonists set sail from England on the *Anne*. They arrived in Charles Town (present-day Charleston, South Carolina) on January 13, 1733. The death of two children en route was the only trouble encountered by the colonists during their entire passage.

Shortly after putting in at Charles Town, Oglethorpe asked Governor Robert Johnson of South Carolina for help in finding a site for his colonists. The people of Charles Town were delighted to be of assistance, because the new settlers would live on land between them and the Spaniards, who had settled in Florida.

From Charles Town, Oglethorpe sailed to Beaufort, South Carolina, where he met with Colonel William Bull, a civil engineer. The rest of the colonists remained in Beaufort while Bull and Oglethorpe sailed down the coast to Tybee Island. Oglethorpe was disappointed to find that Tybee Island was mostly marshland—half water, half land. Bull said he knew of a place at a higher elevation, but it had a disadvantage: an Indian village located near the site served as headquarters for the Yamacraw Indians. Oglethorpe, however, was not discouraged.

When he saw the second site, Oglethorpe believed it was perfect for his settlement. A bluff rose some forty feet above the river. With nearly a mile of frontage on the water, the site offered ample room for a large settlement. Upon further investigation, Oglethorpe discovered a high, dry plain to the south that was covered with pines, live oaks, and magnolias. On the east and west were small creeks and swamps affording excellent drainage. More important, the river was capable of floating ships of ordinary tonnage close enough to the shore to discharge their cargoes easily.

To the north lay the rich delta of the river, with its islands and lowlands crowded with dense growths of cypress, sweet gum, tupelo, and other trees, many of which were vine-covered and draped in Spanish moss. The delicious perfume of yellow jasmine mingled with the fresh scent of pine. The site seemed ideal except for one thing: the Yamacraws.

Realizing that good relations with the neighboring Yamacraws were essential to the colony's survival, Oglethorpe suggested that the colonists call on them as soon as possible.

The chief of the tribe, or "mico," was Tomo-chi-chi. He was six feet tall and as strong as a Georgia oak. Fortunately for Oglethorpe, a half-breed named Mary Musgrove—known as Coosaponakesee among the Indians—lived in the area. Mary was soon enlisted as a translator between Tomo-chi-chi and Oglethorpe. She would exert valuable influence in securing pledges of harmony from Tomo-chi-chi.

At their first meeting, Oglethorpe explained that his colonists desired to settle nearby. He assured Tomo-chi-chi that they would not interfere with the Yamacraws, and that they would trade blankets, hatchets, and guns with them. Tomo-chi-chi believed Oglethorpe and agreed that there was room for both the Yamacraws and the colonists.

After this initial meeting, Oglethorpe and William Bull returned to the expectant colonists with the good news. On February 1, 1733, the colonists landed on the western end of the bluff, from which they could make an easy ascent to the tableland. They erected tents of pine branches, cedars, and evergreen oaks.

Oglethorpe and Bull soon marked out a village square, streets, and lots for homes. On February 10, Oglethorpe wrote that the first house was already under construction. The new town was named Savannah.

After five months of exhaustive work, Oglethorpe was ready to assign homes to the settlers, who had spent the winter and spring in four large tents. The basic organizational unit of the community was to be a "tithing," a concept that originated in Anglo-Saxon villages. Under a system called "frankpledge," a tithing was composed of ten households. Every member of a tithing was answerable for the good conduct of, or the damage done by, any of its members. The man in charge was known as a "tithingman." In later years, these officers became known as parish peace officers or petty constables.

By 1740, there were some 142 houses, huts, and public buildings in Savannah, along with a jail, a store, a wharf, and a courthouse that doubled as a church. Oglethorpe named the wards and tithings for the men who served as the colony's trustees. The new town's squares were named after prominent people in the development of the colony. Although some of the squares have been replaced by modern buildings and parking garages, the ones that remain lend a special ambiance to the city.

Johnson Square, the earliest of Savannah's squares, was named for Robert Johnson, the governor of South Carolina who was so helpful to James Oglethorpe and his colonists when they arrived in Charles Town. The tradition of having a sundial in Johnson Square dates back to colonial days. The current version, sponsored by the Society of Colonial Wars, was completed in 1933 to commemorate the two hundredth anniversary of the founding of Georgia; called the William Bull Sundial, it honors the man who helped choose the site for Savannah and lay out the town.

In days gone by, the Trustees' Store, the Publick Oven, and the Publick Mill fronted this square. They have since been replaced by modern businesses.

One of the early structures on Johnson Square still exists: Christ Episcopal Church. Plans for the original church were drawn as early as 1735, but innumerable delays dragged out the construction for twelve long years. Savannah's original settlers were members of the Church of England, and their church, Christ Church, was considered the mother church of the colony. After the Revolutionary War, the Anglican church in America fell into decline,

Christ Episcopal Chruch

as most of its ministers had been Loyalists. The Anglicans living in the newly independent colonies subsequently organized the Episcopal church, and Christ Church officially became Christ Episcopal Church.

The present structure dates from 1838. It replaced several others on the site that were either razed or burned. The current church itself fell victim to fire in 1898, when its interior was gutted by a blaze. The exterior walls remained sound, however, and the interior was simply rebuilt.

Over the years, Johnson Square has been visited by many important people. On May 12, 1819, President James Monroe attended a ball held in a pavilion constructed in the square. The editor of the *Savannah Republican* called the ball "the most brilliant we ever beheld." Monroe's visit came during a major tour of the Southern states. The crowning event of the entire tour occurred in Savannah, when the president boarded the spectacular new steamship *Savannah* for a trip down the river to Tybee. Before the month was out, the *Savannah* earned lasting fame as the first steam-powered vessel to cross the Atlantic.

A monument to General Nathanael Greene is located at the center of Johnson Square. The general's grave is also on the site.

Nathanael Greene was born to a Quaker family in Rhode Island. However, his interest in military matters led to his eventual expulsion from the pacifist church. When trouble with Great Britain threatened in the 1770s, he organized a company called the Kentish Guards. After the Battle of Lexington, the guards set out to aid the patriot cause. The governor of Rhode Island, being loyal to the British, recalled the guards, but Greene and three other men continued to Boston.

Greene took part in the siege of Boston as a brigadier general in the Continental Army. In 1776, he rose to the rank of major general and commanded the army of occupation in Boston. He later fought with General George Washington at Valley Forge.

Greene ultimately became the leader of patriot forces in the South. He took over from Horatio Gates in December 1780, after the patriots' defeat at Camden, South Carolina. Greene's campaign in the South thwarted Cornwallis and ensured the patriots' success at Yorktown. Many historians rank Greene's importance to the American cause second only to that of George Washington himself.

More than any other commander, Greene was instrumental in freeing Georgia from British occupation. After the war, the newly formed Georgia legislature rewarded his efforts with a plantation known as Mulberry Grove, located 12 miles above Savannah. This handsome estate was the former home of Lieutenant Governor John Graham, who had chosen to support England; after the war, his land was confiscated. Within a few months of receiving the gift, Greene transferred his residence from Newport, Rhode Island, to Savannah, eager to enjoy the balmier climate.

Unfortunately, he only enjoyed his new home a short time. While overseeing his plantation one midsummer day, he was felled by sunstroke. He never rallied, dying on June 19, 1786.

Three days later, all the shops in Savannah closed for his funeral. Military units turned out in full dress, wearing black armbands. Greene's remains were laid to rest in one of the brick vaults in Colonial Park Cemetery.

The monument to Greene was erected in Johnson Square in 1825. The pieces of New York marble that comprise it were shipped to Savannah aboard several vessels. The monument was initially a subject of controversy, drawing unflattering comments from the local citizens. Now, however, it stands as Savannah's most beloved monument, and has served as the site of countless official celebrations.

Over the years, the letters identifying the graves in the vaults at Colonial Park Cemetery disappeared. Those were the days when yellow fever plagued residents of the coastal lowlands; because the cause of the disease was still unknown, officials were reluctant to open the tombs to search for the exact location of Greene's body, fearing contamination. Thus, for 114 years, the tomb of General Greene was lost.

Before his death, Greene had been president of the Rhode Island Society of the Cincinnati, the oldest military organization in the United States, founded in 1783 with George Washington as its first president. In 1902, the Rhode Island Society oversaw a successful search for Greene's exact resting place. The general's remains, along with those of his son, George Washington Greene, were subsequently moved to Johnson Square, where they rest beside the Greene Monument.

Mulberry Grove, Greene's plantation, also played an important role in Southern history. Two years after the general's death, his widow and her plantation superintendent, Phineas Miller, were traveling in the North when they met a young law student who was seeking a position in the South. They hired the student because of his interest in cotton production. This young man was Eli Whitney, the inventor of the cotton gin. He did most of his work on the gin at Mulberry Grove.

From Johnson Square, proceed two blocks south on Bull Street to Wright Square. This square was laid out in 1733 and named for James Wright. Wright served as attorney general of South Carolina for twenty-one years before becoming the last royal governor of Georgia. He was one of the most admired of the colonial governors. In fact, his peers often referred to him as "His Majesty's most able administrator in the Americas." Wright's service to the colony even earned him knighthood.

However, Wright's lofty standing went into a sharp decline at the approach of the Revolution. Georgia had always been the king's most loyal colony; in fact, it was the only colony not to send a delegation to the first Continental Congress. But Savannah finally caught the revolutionary fever. Rebels stole gunpowder and dumped shore batteries over the city's bluff. Governor Wright forbade public meetings, which were held nonetheless.

The crowning blow came in 1775 with the death of two of Wright's strongest allies, Noble Jones and James Habersham. (For more information about Jones and Habersham, see The Wormsloe Tour, pages 75–78; 81–83.) Both men left sons who were leaders in the independence movement, the new generation taking over Savannah. Georgia did indeed send a delegation to the second Continental Congress. Ultimately, Major Joseph Habersham, the son of Wright's old friend, placed the governor under arrest at his mansion. Wright vowed to remain under house arrest, but he quickly broke that promise and fled to the H.M.S. *Scarborough*, which was anchored off Savannah. So ended his governorship of Georgia.

Fortunately, the people of Savannah do not bear grudges. Since that brief period of ill will during the Revolution, Sir James Wright has again been held in high esteem.

In the center of Wright Square stands a monument to William Gordon, founder of the Central of Georgia Railroad.

In the southeastern quadrant of the square is a monument to Tomo-chi-chi, an Indian who was of great help to James Oglethorpe in Georgia's early days.

After Oglethorpe chose the site for his new colony, he invited representatives from nine tribes of the Creek nation, including the Yamacraws, to meet with the colonists in Savannah to negotiate a treaty. The Indians agreed to give the colonists all the land they needed for their comfort and subsistence. In return, the colonists agreed to make restitution for any injuries done to the Indians. This meeting was successful largely because of the influence of Tomo-chi-chi, the chief of the Yamacraws.

Oglethorpe and Tomo-chi-chi became good friends. When Oglethorpe planned a trip to England to report to the trustees on the progress of the settlement, he decided to take some of his new friends with him. The English

Monument to William Gordon at Wright Square

were eager for any morsel of information about the Native Americans. Several Indians, including Tomo-chi-chi, his wife, Scenawki, and his nephew, Toonahowi, were on board when the ship left Savannah on April 7, 1734.

When the vessel reached England, King George and Queen Caroline sent three royal coaches, each drawn by six horses, to bring the guests to the palace. The monarchs were not disappointed by what they saw, for the Indians had painted their faces and attired themselves in beads, feathers, and leather. The English were particularly impressed with Tomo-chi-chi's noble bearing, despite the fact that he was more than ninety years old.

During their stay in England, the visitors were escorted to sites such as Windsor Castle and the Tower of London. They met the archbishop of Canterbury. Oglethorpe finally took them to his country estate for a short visit, just so they could rest and not be on display.

Tomo-chi-chi died in 1739, six years after the founding of the Georgia colony. His last wish was that he be buried among the white men.

Tomo-chi-chi's grave was located at the center of Wright Square, where the monument to William Gordon stands today. James Oglethorpe himself selected the site and erected a pyramid of stone over the Indian's resting place. Over the years, local people somehow came to the mistaken belief that Tomo-chi-chi was buried in the southeastern portion of the square. His actual grave was vandalized, and when the Central of Georgia Railroad asked to build a memorial to William Gordon on that site, no one objected. By the time it became known that the site was actually Tomo-chi-chi's grave, it was too late.

Burial marker for Tomo-chi-chi

In 1899, the Georgia Society of the Colonial Dames of America made the current monument to Tomo-chi-chi one of its first projects.

On the east side of Wright Square is one of Savannah's most celebrated landmarks, the Lutheran Church of the Ascension. The congregation was organized by John Martin Bolzius in 1741. (For more information about Bolzius, see The Salzburger Tour, pages 3, 6.) In 1771, the congregation purchased the lot where the church now stands. In 1772, it erected the first church on this site. This first building burned in 1797 and was replaced by a second church. A portion of the present structure was built in 1843, with the remainder of the construction taking place in the 1870s. Today, the church is one of Savannah's most popular tourist attractions because of its Ascension window and the dramatic interiors of the sanctuary and the other rooms. It is open to the public.

Lutheran Church of the Ascension

After you have seen the Lutheran Church of the Ascension, head south on Bull Street. You will pass the Juliette Gordon Low birthplace on the northeast corner of Oglethorpe Avenue and Bull Street.

This Regency-style mansion was constructed between 1818 and 1821 for Mayor James M. Wayne, who later became a Supreme Court justice. In 1831, Wayne sold the house to his niece, Sarah, and her husband, William Washington Gordon. Members of the Gordon family lived here until 1953.

Juliette Gordon Low, the founder of the Girl Scouts of the U.S.A., was born here on Halloween night in 1860. The house has been restored to how it looked in 1886, the year Juliette was married. Were she around today, she might request that the people of Savannah pick another year, as hers was not the happiest of marriages. After her wedding, Juliette moved to England with her husband, where he proceeded to invite the affections of other women. Juliette was on the brink of filing for divorce when her husband died.

Juliette Gordon Low birthplace

It was during her years abroad that Juliette met Lord Robert Baden-Powell, the founder of the scouting movement for boys in England. From him, she drew the inspiration to launch a similar effort for girls in America. Juliette's new organization, originally called the Girl Guides, began with a meeting of eighteen girls at Juliette's home at 329 Abercorn Street, the Andrew Low House. The first registered member was Juliette's niece, Daisy Gordon Lawrence. From those humble beginnings has grown the major Girl Scouts organization of today.

Juliette Gordon Low died in 1927 and was buried in Laurel Grove Cemetery. The Girl Scouts purchased the home at Oglethorpe and Bull from the Gordon family in 1953. In 1965, the building became Savannah's first National Historic

Landmark. The Juliette Gordon Low Center now serves as a memorial to the organization's founder. It is also the national program center for the Girl Scouts.

Continue on Bull Street for one block to Chippewa Square, which demonstrates local officials' fondness for naming public squares after prominent world events of the day, even if those events had no direct ties to Savannah. Chippewa Square memorializes the Battle of Chippewa, which was fought in Canada during the War of 1812. In July 1814, American forces crossed the Niagara River from Buffalo to defeat the British on Canadian soil. This marked the last attempt by the United States to invade Canada. After holding Fort Erie for several months, the Americans were driven back across the border by superior forces.

A bronze statue of James Oglethorpe stands in the square today. It was designed by Daniel Chester French, considered the dean of American sculptors. Erected in 1910, it is considered the most distinguished of Savannah's statues.

Bronze statue of James Oglethorpe in Chippewa Square

The building at 208 Bull Street on Chippewa Square once housed the historic Chatham Academy, Savannah's first institution for secondary education. The academy's original building, constructed in 1812, was destroyed by fire in 1899. The present building dates from 1908. Classes were held at Chatham Academy until the spring of 1975. The Chatham County Board of Education now owns the building. Today, another school in Savannah goes by the name of Chatham Academy, but it is not at this location. That school serves the needs of children with learning disabilities and has no connection with the historic Chatham Academy.

First Baptist Church is located on the west side of the square. The Baptist tradition in Georgia stretches back to 1763, when the Reverend Nicholas Bedgegood came to Savannah from Charleston to work at the Bethesda Home for Boys and serve as a missionary to James Oglethorpe's colony. That same year, Bedgegood administered the first recorded baptism by immersion in Georgia.

In 1791, the Calvinistic Baptist Society acquired a lot on Washington Square. Four years later, the city exchanged two lots on Franklin Square for the property on Washington Square. The congregation of First Baptist Church was organized in 1800. That year, a small wooden structure was dedicated on the Franklin Square property. It was used until 1833, when the present church building was constructed on Chippewa Square. First Baptist survives as the oldest church building in Savannah. Many distinguished ministers have

served the congregation, including the Reverend Jesse Mercer, who founded Mercer University in Macon, Georgia.

Continue south on Bull Street for two blocks to Madison Square. Laid out in 1839, Madison Square was named for President James Madison. It features a monument to Sergeant William Jasper, one of the heroes of the Battle of Savannah during the Revolutionary War.

The Battle of Savannah is not often grouped with Yorktown, Bunker Hill, and Trenton when crucial moments of the Revolutionary War are discussed. Yet this battle, the climax of which was staged on a small hill just west of what is now downtown on a foggy morning in October 1779, proved so gruesome that one observer called it "an exhibition of . . . barbarous warfare of which details would shock an Arab." Historians consider it a classic confrontation of French and British military skill. Charles-Henri, Compte d'Estaing, the leader of French forces in the West Indies, led the Americans and their allies that day. It was a losing effort. By the end of the clash, the Americans and their allies sustained 752 killed and the British only 57.

During the battle, Sergeant William Jasper was wounded twice but continued fighting for the patriot cause. He finally lost his life while trying to catch the regimental flag as it fell from a broken staff. As a shot pierced his body, he supposedly murmured, "I have got my furlough."

Statue of Sergeant William Jasper

The granite marker which honors Jasper also defines the southern line of the British defense during the battle. (For more information about the Battle of Savannah, see The Old Seaport Tour, pages 52–53.)

On the west side of the square is St. John's Episcopal Church, with the parish house close by on the corner of Bull and Harris streets. The parish house was completed in 1861 after eleven years of construction. Today, it draws attention as the location of General William T. Sherman's headquarters during his stay in Savannah.

After Union troops under Sherman captured Atlanta, they continued their scorched-earth policy, moving toward the Georgia coast in what came to be known as Sherman's "March to the Sea." Woodrow Wilson spent his childhood years in Georgia during the Civil War; in fact, his father, a strong Southern sympathizer, turned his church into a hospital for wounded Confederate soldiers. Wilson remembered Sherman's men this way: "They devoted themselves to destruction, and to the stripping of the land they crossed with a thoroughness and a care of details hardly to be matched in the annals of modern warfare—each soldier played a marauder very heartily."

Upon Sherman's arrival in Savannah, cotton merchant Charles Green invited the general to move into his elegant new home at Bull and Harris streets. That is not to say that Green was sympathetic to Sherman. One of Green's sons was a Confederate soldier, and he himself was once arrested and imprisoned in Boston for importing medical supplies for the Southern cause. Actually, Green was motivated by sympathy for the people of Savannah. Since he was a British citizen, he figured his action would spare some other resident of Savannah the humiliation of having Sherman occupy his home.

Fortunately for Sherman, Green's home may have been the best in town. It was considered a cultural and social center. An English journalist describing Green's home in 1863 said it was graced with Italian statuary, finely carved tables and furniture, and stained glass and portraits from Europe. The bathrooms were luxurious, with a good supply of fresh water. The journalist was surprised to find such elegance in the city.

The Reverend Cameron Farquahar McRae, the pastor of St. John's Episcopal Church since 1862, was a boarder in Green's home. Upon learning that Sherman had accepted Green's invitation to move in, McRae reportedly snapped that he would not live under the same roof with such a man, and promptly departed. The Yankee commander then moved into McRae's room, the front room on the second floor.

On December 21, 1864, only one hour after moving into the house, Sherman sent a famous Christmas message to President Abraham Lincoln: "I beg to present you as a Christmas Gift, the City of Savannah with 150 heavy guns and plenty of ammunition and also about 25,000 bales of cotton."

Sherman remained at the Green mansion for five weeks. During that time, several important people from the North dropped by for visits, but few Savannah natives called on the hated general.

St. John's Episcopal Church

In 1943, St. John's Episcopal Church purchased the house for use as a parish house. Today, the public can tour the home. A niche in the stairway showcases a bust of the Reverend McRae, the man who moved out rather than live in the same house with the enemy.

The neighboring St. John's Episcopal Church is noted for its melodious chimes and its lovely stained-glass windows. Designed by Calvin Otis in the Gothic Revival style, it was built in 1852 and 1853.

Continue south on Bull Street. Monterey Square, the last square on Bull Street, is two blocks from Madison Square.

St. John's Parish House

In the mid-nineteenth century, one of Savannah's proudest military groups was called the Irish Jasper Greens. When the Irish Jasper Greens returned from the Mexican War in 1847, it was decided that a square should be named in honor of their participation in the Battle of Monterey.

Monterey Square exemplifies the pride of Savannah's citizens in commemorating far-flung military ventures. It also bears witness to the rather random organization of some of the city's squares. Pulaski Square, located only a few blocks away, was named in honor of Casimir Pulaski, a hero of the American Revolution. But the city's monument to Pulaski resides in Monterey Square, which commemorates a battle in Mexico.

Casimir Pulaski was a Polish count who joined George Washington's forces. After the Battle of Brandywine in 1777, he was appointed brigadier general in charge of cavalry. The following year, Pulaski organized an independent corps of cavalry and light infantry that became known as Pulaski's Legion. The legion participated in the Battle of Savannah, in which Pulaski was wounded on October 9, 1779. He died two days later.

Monterey Square is surrounded by some of Savannah's finest old homes. Both the Mercer House, located at 429 Bull Street, and the double house at 423-25 Bull Street provide examples of Savannah's best ironwork.

Continue one block south to Gaston Street. Forsyth Park is located straight ahead. This twenty-acre park, designed in 1851, was named for Governor John Forsyth. Forsyth served as secretary of state under both Andrew Jackson and Martin Van Buren.

Pulaski monument

Mercer House

423-25 Bull Street

One of the main features of the park is the spectacular white fountain. Constructed in 1858, it is believed to have been the largest fountain in the nation at that time. Near the fountain is the Fragrant Garden for the Blind, a unique project sponsored by the garden clubs of Savannah. At the northwestern corner of the park, at the junction of Whitaker and Gaston streets, stands the Georgia Historical Society. The building which houses the society was commissioned by the Telfair family, discussed later in this tour.

An impressive monument to the Confederacy is enclosed within iron railings in what is known as Forsyth Park Extension, a former military parade ground. The monument dates from 1875. One of the busts within the iron railings honors Brigadier General Francis S. Bartow.

Wealthy and well-educated, Francis Bartow had a short but spectacular military career, during which he showed a knack for uttering memorable quotes. In January 1861, he was one of three representatives from Savannah at Georgia's secession convention. When Georgia seceded, Bartow led the Oglethorpe Light Infantry to Virginia to join Lee and Beauregard. On his way out of Savannah, he shouted, "I go to illustrate Georgia!"

Bartow met his death during the First Battle of Bull Run, his only engagement with Union forces. While leading the Oglethorpe Light Infantry, he was shot from his horse, remounted, charged again, and was shot a second time, this time through the heart. His final words were these: "They have killed me, boys, but never give up the field." His remains arrived back in Savannah in July 1861, only six months after he had attended the secession convention.

Turn right (west) off Bull Street onto Gaston Street. Proceed two blocks to Barnard Street. Turn right (north) and continue one block to Chatham Square. This square was named for William Pitt, the earl of Chatham. Prior to the Revolutionary War, Pitt protested British policy in the House of Lords. He often spoke eloquently about the British obligation to support English subjects wherever they lived and whatever their circumstances. His speeches were so powerful that law students passed notes to one another in class saying, "Don't miss Parliament. Old Pitt is speaking."

Continue north on Barnard Street for two blocks to Pulaski Square, named for Count Casimir Pulaski. At the northeast corner of the square, at 126-28 West Harris Street, is a three-story house above a raised basement. This beautifully restored home once belonged to Francis Bartow.

Continue north on Barnard Street for two blocks to Orleans Square, named in honor of the Battle of New Orleans. Tensions were high in Savannah during the War of 1812. Patrolling just off the coast, the British navy proved a major interruption to shipping. More important, the citizens had a legitimate fear of invasion. After Andrew Jackson led the Americans to victory at New Orleans,

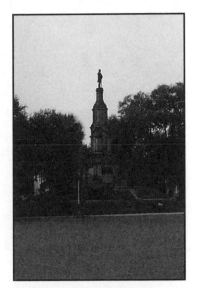

Forsyth Park monument to the Confederacy

Fountain in Forsyth Park

the people of Savannah were understandably relieved. The great irony of that battle was that it took place fifteen days after a treaty of peace had been signed in Belgium. Slow communications prevented word of the treaty from reaching the armies in time to avoid confrontation.

The Champion-McAlpin-Fowlkes House, which faces the square at 230 Barnard Street, is an excellent example of the Greek Revival style. The home was built in 1844 for Aaron Champion, who gave it as a wedding gift to his daughter when she married James McAlpin, the son of one of Savannah's wealthiest citizens, Henry McAlpin.

In 1815, Henry McAlpin came into possession of a hundred acres of land on the Savannah River approximately 1 mile west of what is now the historic district. McAlpin turned this acreage, known as the Hermitage as early as 1763, into a model plantation. In fact, it became the only plantation on the Savannah River to attain prominence through industrial development, rather than agriculture.

Unlike most plantation owners, McAlpin made use of every square foot of his land, planting the low-lying portions in rice and using the higher elevations for lumbering and manufacturing. Brick and iron crafted at the plantation were used throughout the city. McAlpin even built the first railroad in the United States at the Hermitage, a horse-drawn affair designed to move heavy loads from kiln to kiln. The manor house at the Hermitage was noted for its mantels and stairs, which were made of marble imported from Europe. The home was constructed by slaves. By the time he died of heart trouble in 1851, Henry McAlpin had greatly increased his landholdings and was the director of a bank.

Henry Ford later bought the Hermitage manor house, but not the land itself. He had the mansion disassembled and moved to Richmond Hill, south of Savannah, where it was put back together. It now stands on private property and cannot be toured. Ford also bought two slave cabins from the Hermitage property, which he had moved to the Ford Museum at Dearborn, Michigan.

In 1935, the Union Bag and Paper Corporation obtained a ninety-nine-year lease on the old Hermitage property. In a short time, the company erected a huge paper mill on the former plantation. Some of the old buildings were later used by the Diamond Match Company. The area is heavily industrialized today.

The Champion-McAlpin-Fowlkes House is one of the few links to the McAlpin family visible in Savannah today. On the outside, the iron gates, the sandstone steps, and the two-story Corinthian columns all suggest the opulence inside. The front hall has a black marble floor and four square columns around an oval rotunda which rises three stories to a skylight.

Also bordering Orleans Square, on the corner of Montgomery Street and Oglethorpe Avenue, is the Savannah Civic Center.

Proceed north on Barnard Street for two blocks to Telfair Square. This square was known as St. James Square until the city's sesquicentennial in 1883. At that time, the name was changed to honor Edward Telfair, a three-time governor of Georgia, and his daughter Mary, who was Savannah's greatest benefactor during the difficult period following the Civil War.

When Edward Telfair died in 1807, he left his three children—Alexander, Margaret, and Mary—very wealthy. In 1819, Alexander built a mansion at 121 Barnard Street, facing the square; the home was designed by William Jay. In 1875, after the death of Mary Telfair, the last surviving family member, the mansion, its furnishings, its books, and a thousand shares of railroad stock were willed to the Georgia Historical Society.

Telfair Academy of Arts and Sciences

In the 1880s, the mansion was remodeled and enlarged into what became the first art museum in the Southeast. Today, it houses the Telfair Academy of Arts and Sciences, which contains an excellent collection of American, French, and German impressionist paintings. The first painting purchased by the museum, *Relics of the Brave*, hangs in the rotunda gallery, along with Jean-François Raffaelli's *La Demoiselle d'Honneur*.

At the head of the stairs are two ancient Greek capitals that experts have said are identical to stones used in Egyptian temples during the period of Alexander the Great. The story is told that the stones came to Savannah by accident. In the days when sailing vessels used stone for ballast, a load of such material was unloaded on the wharves of Savannah. A local man noticed the unusual stones and took them home. They were used in a home on St. Simons Island and were later presented to the museum.

There is another interesting story about the building. When the Telfairs bequeathed the home to the Georgia Historical Society, they made one request—that no alcoholic beverages ever be served on the premises. This stricture was followed for years, until the management finally relented and served champagne at an art reception. It just so happened that a portion of the roof chose that very moment to cave in on the guests. Although no one was hurt, the legend spread that the Telfair ghosts had let their displeasure be known.

Just south of the Telfair Academy of Arts and Sciences, at 127 Barnard Street, stands Trinity United Methodist Church, the oldest Methodist church in

Trinity United Methodist Church

Savannah. The cornerstone of this church was laid on February 14, 1848. The structure, similar in design to Wesley Chapel of London, is made of gray brick, stucco, and virgin Georgia longleaf pine.

Telfair Square was one of the most prestigious areas of the early colony. When Henry Ellis replaced Captain John Reynolds as governor of the colony in 1757, he selected what was then St. James Square for his home. Joseph Gibbons, a three-time mayor of Savannah and a prominent figure in the development of steam power, also lived here. And Brown's Inn, located on the corner where the Georgia Federal Bank now stands, hosted George Washington in 1791.

Continue north on Barnard Street for two blocks to what used to be Ellis Square.

From its earliest days, Ellis Square was Savannah's marketplace. Market stalls were stacked with products from the plantations and nearby islands. For many years, the square's only competition came from Negro street vendors who peddled seafood door to door through much of the city, carrying big baskets on their heads and filling the air with their famous cry, "Crab by'er! Yeh shrimps! Yeh oysta!" Housewives wanting seafood for their dinner tables kept the custom alive despite the protests of city officials concerned with sanitary food handling. With their buckets of crabs, shrimp, and oysters, and with their baskets of flowers in springtime, the street vendors lent a colorful character to Savannah shopping.

Today, Ellis Square—the old marketplace—is completely covered by a parking garage. The street vendors are gone, too.

One of the early settlers in the neighborhood bordering Ellis Square was Benjamin Sheftall, the leader of a small boatload of Jews who arrived in Georgia in 1733, only a short time after James Oglethorpe and the original colonists.

A misunderstanding was at the root of the Jewish presence in the new colony. One of the organizations that helped raise funds to settle Englishmen in Georgia was Congregation Bevis Marks, a Jewish congregation in London, which planned to send Jews to America as well. Feeling that their people had been mistreated by the Spanish during the Inquisition, many Jews favored establishing a province in America that would oppose Spain. However, the trustees of the colony understood that only Protestants were to be sent to Georgia. When they learned of the arrival of the Jews, they urged James Oglethorpe to drive them out. Oglethorpe disagreed with this policy. He allowed the Jews to stay in Savannah and even granted them minimal tracts of land.

The majority of Jews arriving in Georgia were of Spanish or Portuguese origin. The Sheftall family was among the few of German descent. The industrious Benjamin Sheftall soon attained prominence as a shopkeeper.

Sheftall had two sons, both of whom fought for the patriot cause in the Revolution, and both of whom were captured by the British.

Mordecai Sheftall became a prominent citizen of Savannah after the war. He was one of the major forces behind the building of Chatham Academy.

However, the other son, who bore the unlikely name of Sheftall Sheftall, suffered greatly during the Revolution, the victim of harsh treatment in British prisons in Charleston and the West Indies. He returned from the war with an obsessive patriotism, refusing to wear anything but his Continental Army uniform and tricorn hat. He wore the hat at such a jaunty angle that he acquired the nickname "Cocked Hat" Sheftall. It became his habit to march back and forth, spinning smartly on his heel and saluting frequently, in front of the family home on Ellis Square, in plain view of shoppers in the marketplace.

When the Marquis de Lafayette visited Savannah in 1825 to participate in the dedication of the monument to Nathanael Greene, Cocked Hat Sheftall, dressed in full regalia, was among the soldiers waiting to greet him on the platform.

The day finally came when Sheftall could no longer pay the taxes on his home. In an unprecedented move, the city council passed a resolution in 1841 remitting all his back taxes and overlooking any future ones. When Sheftall Sheftall died on August 15, 1847, his obituary noted that he was "distinguished by his 'Knee-Breeches' and his 'Cocked Hat,' . . . for many years past . . . lingering among us like a sacred leaf from a departed summer."

Proceed around the parking garage to Bryan Street. Turn left, heading west, and continue two blocks to Franklin Square, named for Benjamin Franklin.

Benjamin Franklin is held in deep esteem by the people of Savannah. From 1768 to 1775, he served as the Georgia colony's agent in London; during that period, he sent samples of Chinese rice from London back to Savannah, so aiding the progress of the area's rice culture. When Franklin, back in America, was chosen postmaster general in 1775, he organized the postal service to provide efficient mail delivery from Portland, Maine, to Savannah. He is also remembered with fondness for helping establish what is now the Bethesda Home for Boys. (For more information about Bethesda, see The Wormsloe Tour, pages 80–84.)

The highlight of Franklin Square today is First African Baptist Church, located at 23 Montgomery Street.

First African Baptist Chruch

As early as 1744, a slave named George Leile began making missionary visits to plantations along the Savannah River. On January 20, 1788, his work was rewarded when a permanent congregation of slaves was formed on Brampton Plantation—the oldest African-American congregation in the United States. First African Baptist Church and First Bryan Baptist Church, the latter dating from 1873, evolved from this congregation. First African Baptist Church was formed in the early years of the nineteenth century; in 1826, the first African-American Sunday school in the United States was formed there. The present building dates from 1861.

After their day's labor on the plantation, slaves were allowed to go to the future site of First African Baptist Church and work on its construction. It is said they would walk toward the construction with bowed heads and return after their work proud and uplifted. A hidden room in the basement of the church housed runaway slaves on occasion.

Turn right on Montgomery Street and travel one block to Bay Street. Turn right (east) onto West Bay. Continue ten blocks to the corner of East Bay and Houston. Turn right onto Houston and proceed one block to Washington Square.

The area that was to become Washington Square was the site of a rousing celebration in honor of America's independence. The celebration was held on August 10, 1776. It would have been held on the Fourth of July, but slow communications delayed the news about the signing of the Declaration of Independence. During the celebration, the Declaration was read four separate times, at the insistence of the progressively larger crowds.

Washington Square was organized in 1791. For many years, it served as the site of some of Savannah's largest celebrations. During the first half of this century, it hosted some memorable New Year's Eve parties, with crowds starting bonfires whose flames reached higher than the surrounding buildings.

Turn right (west) on St. Julian Street. It is two blocks to Warren Square.

This square was named for Joseph Warren, a leading statesman before the Revolutionary War. Warren, a Massachusetts resident, drafted some of the key protests against British laws. In 1775, he was elected president of the provincial assembly and was named major general of the Massachusetts forces, a position he held until he became one of the first casualties of the war at the Battle of Bunker Hill.

The people of Massachusetts, and Boston in particular, formed a strong bond with the people of Savannah during the early stages of the struggle for independence. Shortly after the news of the Boston Tea Party reached Savannah, several Savannah residents defied Governor Wright's edict against seditious meetings. On August 10, 1774, the Savannah branch of the Sons of Liberty gathered in Tondee's Tavern, which was located at the corner of Broughton and Whitaker streets, five blocks west of where Warren Square stands today. At that meeting, the Savannah group resolved to aid the Bostonians by sending money and rice.

Almost ninety years later, the people of Boston sent supplies and food to Savannah after Sherman's occupation during the Civil War. The relief supplies were accompanied by a note bearing these words: "The history of former days is not forgotten. It has rather been deepened by the later trials of our nation. We remember the earlier kindness and liberality of the citizens of Savannah towards the people of Boston in the dark colonial days."

Continue two blocks west to Reynolds Square, named for Georgia's first royal governor, Captain John Reynolds. Reynolds came to Georgia in the mid-1750s with high expectations. The people of Savannah welcomed his arrival with an elaborate party. Unfortunately, Reynolds mangled the affairs of Georgia so badly that he was recalled less than two years later.

Statue of John Wesley in Reynolds Square

In the center of the square is a statue of religious leader John Wesley, the founder of Methodism. (For an account of John Wesley's frustrating stay in Georgia, see The Tybee Light Tour, pages 67–68.)

Reynolds Square was once bordered by some of Savannah's finest buildings, including the John Wesley Hotel, the Lucas Theater, and The Filature. The Filature, a long, wooden warehouse, burned in 1758, was rebuilt, and burned again in 1840. Savannah's first major building, it was designed to be the processing center of Georgia silk, but over the course of its life, it also served as a government meeting place, a gunpowder warehouse, and a theater. When George Washington made his tour of the Low Country in 1791, The Filature was the site of a gala given in his honor. The outdoor area behind The Filature was Savannah's dueling place.

One structure on Reynolds Square that has survived from Savannah's early days is the Pink House, located at 23 Abercorn Street. This Georgian-style house was built in 1789 for James Habersham, Jr., the son of one of the founders of the Bethesda Home for Boys. Throughout much of its life, it served as a bank building, including a tenure as a branch of the United States Bank beginning in 1818. Today, the structure houses one of Savannah's best-known restaurants. Employees of the restaurant tell stories of visits from the ghost of James

The Pink House

Owens-Thomas House

TOURING THE COASTAL GEORGIA BACKROADS

Habersham, Jr. At times, candles flame up by themselves, and cold drafts are sometimes felt on warm evenings. One cook even swears that Habersham appears when the food is not prepared to his standards.

Turn left on Abercorn Street. It is two blocks to Oglethorpe Square, named for Savannah's founder. This area was once the home of many of Savannah's finest families. One of the loveliest homes on the square, the Owens-Thomas House, located at 124 Abercorn, is open to the public. Built between 1816 and 1819, this home was designed by William Jay and is an excellent example of the Regency period. It features a columned entrance portico, a winding double stairway, a paneled parapet above the main cornice, and arched second-story windows. The Marquis de Lafayette stayed at this house during a visit in 1825.

Turn left on East York Street. It is two blocks to Columbia Square.

Isaiah Davenport House Museum

The brightest jewel on this square is the Isaiah Davenport House Museum, located at 324 State Street. This imposing Federal-style mansion was completed in 1820 by its namesake, Isaiah Davenport, a master builder and city alderman. But by the 1930s, the grand house had become a tenement, divided into many small apartments. Oilcloth covered the filthy floors, bare bulbs hung from electric cords, and wallpaper hung in tatters. By 1955, plans were under way to demolish the structure to make way for a parking lot. A group of outraged ladies raised over $22,000 to save the house, and the Historic Savannah Foundation was born. The Historic Savannah Foundation has since come to the rescue of numerous other worthy structures around the city.

In the basement of the Isaiah Davenport House is the foundation's museum shop, which features specialty items unique to Savannah and to Isaiah Davenport's time.

Continue east on East York Street for two more blocks to Greene Square. This square, laid out in 1799, was named for Revolutionary War hero Nathanael Greene.

Turn right on Houston Street. It is two blocks to Crawford Square.

This square, the only one in Savannah devoted to public recreation, was named for native son William Harris Crawford, a brilliant political figure in his younger days. Crawford very well could have—should have—been president of the United States. He served as James Madison's secretary of the treasury, and later as Madison's minister to France while Napoleon was emperor. It was said that Crawford was the only foreign envoy with any influence over Napoleon. Some even considered him the most respected man in America.

When Madison was nearing the end of his second term, most political observers expected that Crawford would be his successor. Crawford, in his

Gazebo at Crawford Square

Colonial Park Cemetery

early forties, was a young man with a long future ahead of him. Madison, however, asked him to delay his run for the nation's highest office in favor of James Monroe. Crawford agreed to do so, assuming his position would be just as strong after Monroe's years in the White House.

Unfortunately, just before the end of Monroe's term, Crawford suffered an illness that left him partially paralyzed. Although he recovered enough to run in the 1824 election, he was not the sure bet for the presidency he had been in 1816. He was not up to his former physical strength, and the voters had doubts about his future health. In the election, none of the four candidates—Henry Clay, John Quincy Adams, Andrew Jackson, and Crawford—obtained a majority of votes in the general election. As a result, the election was thrown into the House of Representatives. The House chose Adams, with Crawford running third behind Andrew Jackson. Crawford subsequently retired from national politics and became a circuit judge in Georgia until his death in 1834.

Turn right on McDonough Street and proceed two blocks to Habersham. Turn right and continue a block and a half to Oglethorpe. Turn left. It is two blocks to the entrance to Colonial Park Cemetery, on the left at the corner of Oglethorpe and Abercorn.

This area, opened in 1750, served as a burial place for a hundred years. Many of the city's most famous citizens are buried here.

During Sherman's occupation of Savannah, several corps of his troops camped in Colonial Park Cemetery. The soldiers despoiled and broke many of the headstones. Dozens of grave sites were lost, never to be found again. Modern-day visitors can still see many of the broken markers, now cemented against the cemetery's eastern wall.

When you have enjoyed Colonial Park Cemetery, turn left off Oglethorpe onto Abercorn. It is four blocks to Lafayette Square. This square was named for the Marquis de Lafayette, who visited Savannah in 1825 to lay the cornerstone for the Nathanael Greene Monument in Johnson Square. Twelve years later—two years after the death of the marquis—the city added this square in his honor.

The grand house facing the square at 329 Abercorn belonged to Andrew Low, a wealthy Englishman. Low's son married Juliette Gordon, the founder of the Girl Scouts.

Another famous resident of the neighborhood was Flannery O'Connor, the well-known novelist and short-story writer. O'Connor referred to the townhouse at 207 East Charlton Street as "the house I was raised in." Born in Savannah in 1925, O'Connor lived here until 1938. She died in 1964 at the age of thirty-nine.

The Andrew Low House

Flannery O'Connor's house

Despite the briefness of her career, she won three O'Henry Awards for the best short story of the year and the National Book Award in 1972 for her collected stories. The townhouse is open to the public on weekends.

O'Connor was a member of the Cathedral of St. John the Baptist, the oldest Roman Catholic church in Georgia, which also adjoins Lafayette Square.

Initially, Catholicism was banned in the colony. The first Irish Catholics arrived in Savannah as indentured servants. The congregation of St. John the Baptist was organized in the latter part of the eighteenth century; among its many other affects, the Revolutionary War changed attitudes toward Catholics. In 1876, a magnificent French-Gothic cathedral was dedicated. That structure was destroyed by fire in 1898, but the current church was rebuilt from the original design.

Since the first St. Patrick's Day celebrations in Savannah in the early 1800s, the status of Catholics has swung 180 degrees. Today, the city hosts the second-largest St. Patrick's Day parade in the United States, as determined by the total number of participants. It trails only New York City. Savannah's celebration is also the third-oldest in the country, behind only New York and Boston. And with 20 percent of its citizens claiming Irish ancestry, Savannah can claim a greater percentage of Irishmen than either of those cities.

The celebration begins with a colorful local touch, when the mayor pours green dye into each of the city's fountains, causing the "greening of the fountains." It is joked that even the grits are green in Savannah on St. Patrick's

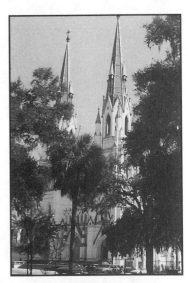

Cathedral of St. John the Baptist

Armillary Sphere *at Troup Square*

Day. These days, it seems nearly everyone in town claims some degree of "Irishness." Not only do the traditional Irish and Scotch-Irish turn out on St. Patrick's Day, but Black-Irish, Greek-Irish, Oriental-Irish, and Spanish-Irish as well.

Turn left off Abercorn onto Charlton. It is two blocks to Troup Square. This square was named for George Michael Troup, who served as congressman, governor, and senator during his illustrious political career.

In the center of the square stands the *Armillary Sphere*, the only modern sculpture on public display in Savannah. A contemporary piece representing ancient thought, it created quite a stir when it was erected, with its circular black bands and its representation of the twelve symbols of the zodiac.

What is informally known as the "Jingle Bells Church" is located at Troup Square. James Pierpont, the composer of "Jingle Bells," served as the music director of this church in the 1850s, when it was a Unitarian church located on Oglethorpe Square. James Pierpont was the brother of the Reverend John Pierpont, Jr., the minister of the Unitarian church. (For more information on James and John Pierpont, see The Old Seaport Tour, pages 53–54.)

Today, the white stucco building serves as The Baptist Center, which conducts worship services on Sunday and during the week.

Troup Square, like Whitefield and Lafayette squares, is surrounded by rows of townhouses featuring various architectural styles.

Gazebo at Whitefield Square

Turn right onto Habersham. It is two blocks to Whitefield Square. This square was named for George Whitefield, the great Methodist evangelist. (For more information on Whitefield, see The Wormsloe Tour, pages 81–83.)

Visitors find the townhouses around Whitefield Square particularly enjoyable—their balconies, iron balustrades, graceful doorways, bay windows, and porticoes. Whitefield Square itself has a Victorian feeling. The houses that border it are enhanced with gingerbread filigree. Most of the townhouses are of stucco and brick, constructed high off the ground, their steps adorned with wrought-iron railings. In the center of the square is a gazebo where band concerts are occasionally held.

Turn right onto Taylor. It is two blocks to Calhoun Square, which memorializes John C. Calhoun, the fiery politician who championed states' rights prior to the Civil War. Calhoun served as a senator from his native state of South Carolina, as secretary of war under James Monroe, and as vice president under John Quincy Adams and Andrew Jackson. This square was dedicated to him in 1851, one year after his death.

On the southeast corner of Abercorn and Gordon streets stands the Massie Heritage Interpretation Center. This is the only original building remaining from Georgia's oldest chartered school system. The building, with its gabled roof, wood cupola and cornice, and unique connecting passageway, was designed by John S. Norris in 1856.

Also on Calhoun Square is Wesley Monumental United Methodist Church, organized in 1875. The church was built to honor John and Charles Wesley. (For more information about Charles Wesley, see The Marshes of Glynn Tour, page 135–136.) The beige stucco building was completed in 1890.

This tour of Savannah's squares ends at Calhoun Square. You may combine this tour with any of several others if you desire to see more of the attractions in the Savannah area.

Wesley Monumental United Methodist Church

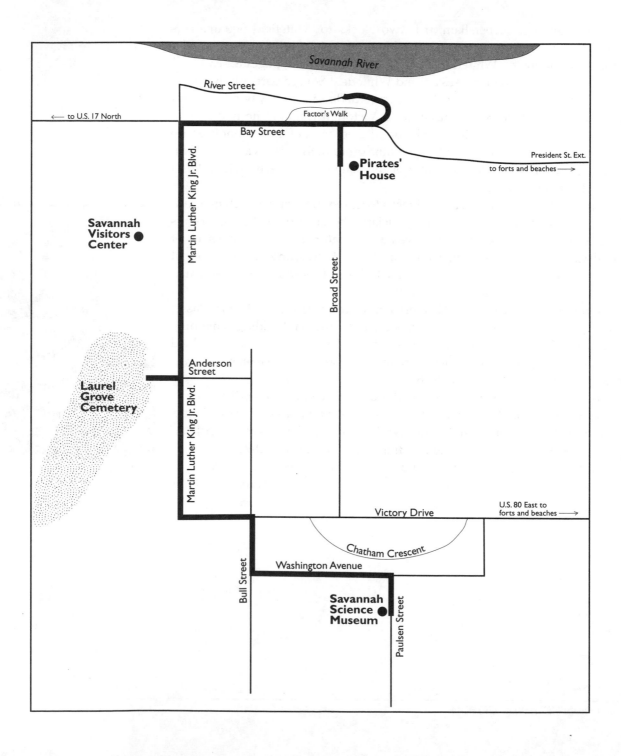

The Old Seaport Tour

This tour makes a counterclockwise circle around the main part of Savannah's historic district, covering areas to the northeast, north, west, and south of the downtown area. It begins at Trustees' Garden Village, on the eastern edge of downtown. A walking tour along River Street and Factor's Walk follows. The tour then continues to the western edge of downtown to the Scarbrough House, the Savannah Visitors Center, and Laurel Grove Cemetery. It ends by exploring Ardsley Park-Chatham Crescent, one of Savannah's most attractive neighborhoods, and the Savannah Science Museum.

Total mileage:
approximately 6 miles.

The tour begins on East Broad Street near the Savannah River in the beautifully restored area known as Trustees' Garden Village.

When the British established Georgia as the thirteenth American colony in 1733, they planned for it to serve as a military buffer between the twelve other colonies to the north and the hostile Spaniards in Florida. They also had another goal for the new colony. As Britain's southernmost American colony, Georgia had the warmest climate and longest growing season. The trustees were counting on Georgia for the cultivation of commodities that England was importing at great expense, especially silk, olive oil, and wine.

To accomplish this goal, James Oglethorpe marked off a ten-acre plot where the colonists were to experiment to find the plants and trees best suited to the soil and climate of the new region. Trustees' Garden, as it was called, became North America's first experimental botanical garden. Botanists were sent all over the world to gather cuttings for the garden, which was modeled after the Chelsea Botanical Garden in London. Trustees' Garden soon sported cuttings of various vines, fruit trees, flax, spices, cotton, indigo, olives, and medicinal herbs. It was in this garden that Georgia's famed peach and cotton crops had their humble beginnings in the mid-eighteenth century.

Part of Trustees' Garden Village, the houses numbered 36 to 56 East Broad Street still feature small gardens today. You can catch a glimpse of them through the ironwork. The charming homes in Trustees' Garden Village date from the early nineteenth century.

The Pirates' House, located at 20 East Broad Street and now serving as a restaurant, is an interesting part of Savannah's seafaring history. Built as a tavern in 1794 and located only a block from the river, it soon attracted seafarers and became a rendezvous location for sailors and pirates.

In fact, it is said that some of the events which inspired Robert Louis

Historical marker for Trustees' Garden

Stevenson to write *Treasure Island* took place in this tavern. The spirit of old Captain Flint from Stevenson's book supposedly roams the portion of the restaurant known as "The Captain's Room." Flint allegedly died in this room, and waiters today tell of ghostly sounds and rattling dishes, which they attribute to the old captain's ghost.

The Pirates' House survives today as a historic restaurant. Among its maze of rooms are remnants of bygone days, including nautical displays and curio collections. One of the dining rooms within the Pirates' House is known as "The Herb House." Identifiable by its walls of oversized bricks painted white, this may be the oldest room in Savannah. The candles on the tables in The Herb House remain lit even at midday, as very little natural light can enter the room.

The parking lot of the Pirates' House gives access to a portion of the old Trustees' Garden not visible from the street.

After viewing the Pirates' House, turn right onto Bay Street, heading downhill, then left onto River Street, which runs along the harbor front. River Street is cobblestone, with a railroad track down its center. You will be better off avoiding the bumpy ride and enjoying a nice stroll among the restaurants, pubs, and unique shops housed in the nineteenth-century cotton warehouses along the water. Plenty of parking space is available to the right of River Street in lots along the river, with other spots located on the "ramps" leading up to Bay Street and the shopping area known as Factor's Walk. If you make the entire loop along River Street, you can enjoy approximately 1.6 miles of walking.

The Pirates' House

As you begin your walk along River Street, the first attraction you will see is a sculpture entitled *Savannah's Waving Girl*. Created by Felix De Weldon in 1971, this sculpture honors Florence Martus, who lived from 1869 to 1943. The inscription reads, "Her immortality stems from her friendly greeting to passing ships, a welcome to strangers entering the port and a farewell to wave them safely onward."

Shops on River Street

In 1887, young Florence, the sister of the lighthouse keeper on nearby Elba Island, met and fell in love with a seafaring man, or so the story goes. Their romance soon led to a proposal of marriage. The sailor promised Florence he would give up the sea after one last voyage. As his ship cruised out of the Savannah River into the open ocean, Florence waved a white handkerchief in farewell from the lighthouse.

Unfortunately, the sailor was lost at sea during that voyage. Florence had supposedly promised her lover that she would greet every ship that passed the lighthouse until he returned. Though the sailor was never to keep his end of the bargain, Florence decided to keep hers. For nearly fifty years, people traveling into or out of Savannah were greeted by a lovely woman standing in front of a home on Elba Island. By day, she greeted travelers by waving a white handkerchief; by night, she signaled with a lantern. During the late nineteenth century and the early part of the twentieth century, the only transportation to and from the islands around Charleston, Beaufort, and Savannah was by boat, so Florence had plenty of ships to keep her busy.

Sculpture on River Street entitled **Savanah's Waving Girl** *by Felix De Weldon*

Her vigil ended in 1931, when her brother retired as lighthouse keeper. He and Florence moved away. In 1938, Florence was invited back to Savannah for a huge celebration attended by three thousand people. She was presented with a large birthday cake decorated to look like her former home on Elba Island. Noting that she had endeared herself to countless travelers over a great period of time, officials on that occasion thought it fitting to dub her the "Sweetheart of Mankind."

A stroll along River Street will allow you to browse souvenir shops, boutiques, shell shops, country stores, pubs, cafes, candy stores, and other interesting establishments. The stores are on the left. On the right, tour boats offer special tours of the harbor. You will see tugboats tied up awaiting their next call. And if you're lucky, you might even see sleek yachts owned by celebrities.

A small park on the right offers comfortable benches if you just want to sit and watch the activity in the harbor.

After strolling along River Street as far as you wish, head uphill to Factor's Walk to enjoy the shops on that level.

Factor's Walk on Bay Street

"Factors" were agents who sold cotton, rice, and other goods for the plantation owners. Every planter did business with a factor. Some planters had their own vessels to transport their products, while others rented boats when they needed to ship products to the factors. When the products reached Savannah, they were stored in these waterfront warehouses until the factors made arrangements with buyers. For years, cotton was the principal commodity passing through the buildings on Factor's Walk. The era after that brought heavy traffic in naval stores.

Stroll eastward along Factor's Walk—back toward the Pirates' House—to return to your car. You will soon come upon Savannah City Hall, which sits astride Factor's Walk; its main entrance is at the foot of Bay Street. This domed building, erected in 1905, is located opposite the spot where the S.S. *Savannah* pulled out of the harbor to embark upon the first successful steam crossing of the Atlantic Ocean. The *Savannah* left harbor on May 22, 1819, and reached Liverpool, England, twenty-seven days later. The date of her departure is celebrated as National Maritime Day. Before she sailed, President James Monroe inspected the vessel and took a trial excursion.

Historical markers commemorating the *Savannah* and the *John Randolph*, the first successful ironclad vessel in American waters, stand near the entrance to city hall.

Farther along Factor's Walk are two cannons displayed in a shelter by the street. These were captured when Lord Cornwallis surrendered at Yorktown. In the 1790s, George Washington presented them as a gift to the Chatham Artillery to show his appreciation for their role in celebrating his tour of the Georgia coast. Over the years, the guns have thundered their welcome to honored city guests, including James Monroe, the Marquis de Lafayette, James K. Polk, Millard Fillmore, Chester A. Arthur, Jefferson Davis, Grover Cleveland, William McKinley, William H. Taft, and Franklin Roosevelt.

Across the street from the cannons is the United States Custom House, one of the most noteworthy buildings in Savannah.

In the early days of the colony, a widow by the name of Overend owned a small house on this site. James Oglethorpe rented that house for his residence during his stays in Savannah.

The colony's first house of worship, known as the Tabernacle and Court House, stood at the rear of the lot presently occupied by the United States Custom House. It was in that church on March 7, 1736, that John Wesley delivered his first sermon in America. (For more information on John Wesley, see The Tybee Light Tour, page 67–68.)

The United States Custom House was completed in 1852. So well preserved is the building that many visitors have difficulty believing it is over 140 years old. It is said that the great granite columns haven't settled even a fraction of an inch since their installation, and that the entire building hasn't developed even the smallest crack.

The mighty columns, estimated at fifteen to twenty tons each, were shipped all the way from Massachusetts aboard sailing vessels. It is said that it took an entire month to move each of the columns up from the river to the construction site, and another month to raise each column into position.

Another notable feature of the building is the winding staircase in the main lobby. Although the steps are made of solid stone, they are locked into each other in such a way that they are entirely unsupported except for where they are attached to the wall.

The United States Custom House has seen its share of Savannah history. During the nineteenth century, federal court facilities were housed on the third floor of the building. In 1860, the court hosted a famous trial involving the yacht *Wanderer*, a slave vessel. That trial marked America's last case against the importation of slaves.

Beyond the guns opposite the United States Custom House is a historical marker commemorating a structure known as the "Coffee House" in late colonial days. In 1785, the state legislature met here. One of the pieces of legislation enacted during that term called for the "establishment of a public seat of learning in this state." Thus, the building once located on this site was the birthplace of the University of Georgia.

Among the attached buildings stretching before you on your left is the Savannah Cotton Exchange.

Sea-island cotton was brought to Georgia from the Bahamas in 1786. It was responsible for much of Georgia's agricultural success in the nineteenth century. Its long fibers didn't stick to its seeds, and it was easier to harvest than shorter-fiber cotton.

Savannah Cotton Exchange

Chartered with forty members, the Cotton Exchange was formed in 1872 to promote the interests of cotton merchants. It also settled disputes, regulated prices, and coordinated services. Thanks to the presence of the cotton industry, Factor's Walk became the Wall Street of Savannah. The Cotton Exchange building was completed in 1887, when Savannah ranked second to none among the world's cotton seaports.

Cotton gradually faded from the scene. With the invasion of the boll weevil, production of sea-island cotton ceased altogether.

City Exchange Bell

Savannah City Hall

Beginning in the latter part of the nineteenth century, another major industry, naval stores, arose to replace it. By 1889, Savannah's naval-stores industry, also headquartered in the Cotton Exchange, was among the greatest in the world. The Cotton Exchange finally closed in 1920.

Before you leave the Cotton Exchange, note the fountain in the form of a winged lion in front of the building. The fountain is surrounded by an ornate iron fence that features medallions of famous statesmen, authors, and poets, shown in profile. Thomas Jefferson, William Prescott, and Joseph Addison are among its notables.

Beyond the Cotton Exchange is a white gazebo which houses the old City Exchange Bell. Bearing the date 1802, this is supposedly the oldest bell in Georgia. Imported from Amsterdam, it hung in the cupola of the City Exchange—the predecessor of Savannah City Hall—from 1804 until the building was razed to make way for the present city hall in 1905. In its day, the bell signaled the closing time for shopkeepers and served as an alarm when fires broke out.

As you continue your stroll along Factor's Walk, note the gas lamps, the catwalks shaded by palmettos and oaks, and the sea gulls wobbling along the sidewalk. You will soon see Savannah's Vietnam Veterans Memorial, a sculpture of gun, boots, and helmet made of white marble. The sculpture is surrounded by anchors that lie scattered at random.

Beyond the Vietnam Veterans Memorial is the Chatham Artillery Memorial. With more than two hundred years under its belt, the Chatham Artillery can

Vietnam Veterans Memorial

boast the longest continuous service of any field artillery unit in the South. Organized in 1786, the unit saw its first duty when it participated in the funeral services for General Nathanael Greene. Since then, it has performed combat duty in nearly every major American conflict, beginning with the Oconee wars between 1789 and 1793. It provided escort for George Washington during his 1791 visit; Washington awarded the unit by presenting it with two cannons captured at Yorktown, still on display in the small shelter across from the United States Custom House, visited earlier in this tour.

Chatham Artillery Memorial

During the Civil War, the Chatham Artillery saw action in Charleston, Florida, and various other places.

In this century, the unit fought Pancho Villa at the Mexican border, the kaiser's men in France during World War I, and Hitler's troops in Europe in World War II, landing at Omaha Beach in February 1944.

The memorial on Factor's Walk was dedicated in 1986 on the unit's two hundredth anniversary.

At the end of Factor's Walk, along Emmet Park, is the Ships of the Sea Museum, which has entrances on both River and Bay streets. This museum offers a large collection of model ships and memorabilia from two thousand years of maritime history. Exhibits include a carpenter shop, a chandlery, and an export display. A modest admission fee is charged.

The Old Harbor Light is located in Emmet Park. This beacon was erected in 1858 as a navigational aid for ships traveling on the Savannah River. Standing seventy-seven feet above river level, it was illuminated by gas.

Old Harbor Light

At this point, return to your car and begin driving the rest of the tour. Head west on Bay Street. It is 0.7 mile from the Ships of the Sea Museum to the intersection with Martin Luther King, Jr., Boulevard. Turn left, or south, and drive a block and a half to the Scarbrough House, located at 41 King Boulevard.

This house was built in 1819 for William Scarbrough, one of the chief investors in the *Savannah*, the steamship mentioned earlier in this tour. In its early days, the tan stucco mansion was a social mecca; President James Monroe stayed here during his visit to the city in 1819. From 1878 to 1972, the building housed a public school for children of African descent. It was designated a National Historic Landmark in 1974. Today, it is owned by the Telfair Academy of Arts and Sciences. It is not open to the public.

After viewing the Scarbrough House, continue on King Boulevard for four and a half blocks to the Savannah Visitors Center, on the right. This huge brick building, once the site of the Central of Georgia Railroad station, also houses the Savannah Chamber of Commerce and the Savannah History Museum.

Ships of the Sea Museum

The Scarbough House

During the Revolutionary War, what is now the parking lot at the visitors center was the site of the heaviest action during the Battle of Savannah.

The British captured Savannah in December 1778. One of the most noteworthy victims of their occupation was John A. Treutlen, Georgia's first governor under the new state constitution. Driven out of Savannah, Treutlen took up refuge in South Carolina. One day, there came a knock on his door from a group of men asking for food. He opened the door, only to discover that the visitors were Tories in disguise. They quickly captured Treutlen and drew and quartered him in front of his family. A Georgia county was later named after the unfortunate governor, but his unknown grave still resides somewhere in the state of South Carolina.

Immediately after capturing Savannah, the British began strengthening their fortifications. In an effort to help the patriots regain the city, the French joined forces with them, dispatching Charles-Henri, Compte d'Estaing, to help the Americans. A joint attack to retake Savannah was planned by d'Estaing and Count Casimir Pulaski, the leader of the American forces.

Between September 3 and October 20, 1779, the French and American forces repeatedly charged the British line of defense. Each time, they were driven back, and the siege was ultimately unsuccessful. The Americans and French suffered considerable casualties, among them Count Pulaski and Sergeant William Jasper. (For more information about Count Pulaski, Sergeant Jasper, and the Battle of Savannah, see The Lincoln's Christmas Gift Tour, pages 27–28.)

Before leaving the visitors center complex, be sure to visit the Savannah History Museum; its entrance is off the visitors center lobby.

As you enter the museum, you will be directed into a small, comfortable theater for a short film on the founding of the Georgia colony, narrated by an actor portraying James Oglethorpe. After the film, you can browse among the exhibits, which include a Central of Georgia steam engine, conductor's clothing, bales of cotton, and other displays representative of old-time Georgia.

You may also want to visit the Historic Railroad Shops Museum, located a block farther along King Boulevard, but still within the visitors center complex.

This is the only surviving pre-Civil War railroad complex of such scale in the country. The site's five acres contain twelve buildings devoted to the construction and maintenance of locomotives and rolling stock. Many old railroad cars and cabooses are on display, but the most interesting exhibit is probably the Central of Georgia Railroad's roundhouse, which operated from 1852 to 1963. The roundhouse is a circular building divided into repair stalls, with a train track laid on the floor of each stall. A round turntable inside the roundhouse also has a track on its floor. When an engine needed repair, it was driven onto the turntable. Once it was decided which stall would be used for the repairs, the turntable was rotated until its track was in line with that particular stall. The engine was then moved from the turntable into the repair stall. When the repairs were completed, the process was reversed.

Continue on King Boulevard for 0.8 mile and turn right onto Anderson Street. Drive two blocks to the end of Anderson, where you will enter Laurel Grove Cemetery.

Laurel Grove Cemetery is one of Savannah's oldest burial grounds. Some 610 Confederate soldiers are buried here, many of whom died at Gettysburg. Among the Confederate dead are four generals: Francis Bartow, J. F. Gilmer, LaFayette McLaws, and Moxley Sorrel. Signs in the cemetery direct visitors to the graves of celebrated people buried here, but you might want to take time to enjoy the detailed ornamentation on the grave markers of even the lesser-known occupants.

One of the graves noted by the signs is that of James Pierpont. Although the name may not be immediately recognizable, his contribution to the world is. He was the composer of the song "Jingle Bells."

Burial site of James Pierpont

James Pierpont came to Savannah as a young widower to join his brother, the Reverend John Pierpont, Jr., the minister at a Unitarian church on Oglethorpe Square. The brothers grew estranged because John did not approve of James's choice of career as a songwriter. James wrote popular songs in much the same fashion as Stephen Foster. Although many of his compositions were well received during their time, the only one that has proven of lasting popularity is "Jingle Bells."

James and John also had a famous nephew. Their sister Juliet married Junius S. Morgan and in 1837 gave birth to the well-known financier John Pierpont Morgan.

Another frequently visited grave in Laurel Grove Cemetery is that of Juliette Gordon Low, the founder of the Girl Scouts. A great many Girl Scouts make pilgrimages to Savannah, and they often place tokens of their visits upon Juliette's grave. (For more information about Juliette Gordon Low, see The Lincoln's Christmas Gift Tour, page 25–26.)

After visiting Laurel Grove Cemetery, return to King Boulevard and turn right. Proceed 0.7 mile to Victory Drive and turn left. After 0.3 mile, turn right on Bull Street.

You are now entering Ardsley Park-Chatham Crescent, a spectacular residential area bordered by Bull Street on the west, Fifty-fourth Street on the south, Waters Avenue on the east, and Victory Drive on the north. Built in the prosperous period from 1910 to the onset of the Great Depression, the area features tree-lined streets, large lots, terraced lawns, and magnificent homes that will remind you of Italian villas, Greek mansions, and Spanish and Gothic castles. James Oglethorpe's ideal of city planning was continued here, with shaded squares in Ardsley Park and circles, a mall, and a landscaped crescent design in Chatham Crescent. The entire area is listed on the National Register of Historic Places as a historic district.

After three blocks on Bull Street, turn left on Washington Avenue, one of the finest streets in Savannah. Travel 0.8 mile through the tunnel of oak trees, then turn right on Paulsen Street. It is approximately 0.8 mile on Paulsen to the Savannah Science Museum, on the right.

In 1953, the American Association of University Women built this natural history museum for the city. It has been expanded several times since. The Savannah Science Museum contains one of the largest reptile and amphibian collections in the Southeast, featuring over 180 species of snakes, lizards, turtles, alligators, salamanders, frogs, and toads, all of which are native to Georgia. The museum also offers collections of shells, fossils, rocks, and

Burial site of Juliette Low

minerals, along with a Foucault pendulum and a planetarium. This is a favorite spot among science-minded children, whether during the school year or in the summer months.

This tour ends at the Savannah Science Museum. If you are interested in seeing more of the city and its environs, it may be combined with any of several other tours.

The Savannah Science Museum

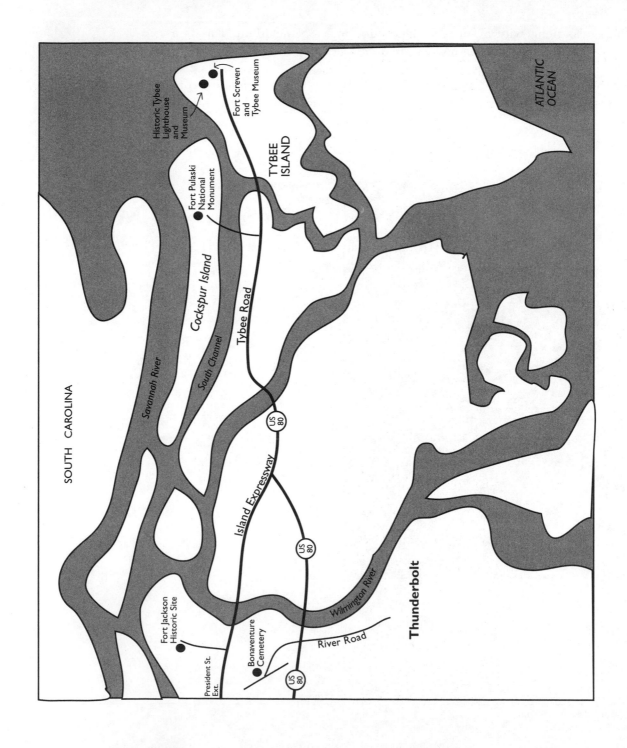

ATLANTIC OCEAN

SOUTH CAROLINA

Savannah River

Cockspur Island

South Channel

Tybee Road

Historic Tybee Lighthouse and Museum

Fort Screven and Tybee Museum

TYBEE ISLAND

Fort Pulaski National Monument

Island Expressway

US 80

US 80

US 80

Wilmington River

Thunderbolt

River Road

Fort Jackson Historic Site

President St. Ext.

Bonaventure Cemetery

The Tybee Light Tour

This tour explores the area east of Savannah. It begins in the town of Thunderbolt, visits Bonaventure Cemetery, and travels to Old Fort Jackson Historic Site and Fort Pulaski National Monument. The tour ends at the Tybee Island Lighthouse.

Total mileage: approximately 25 miles.

The small town called Thunderbolt occupies both banks of the Wilmington River east of Savannah. In fact, Victory Drive (also designated U.S. 80/GA 26) is so heavily trafficked between Savannah and Thunderbolt that you probably wouldn't even notice you were passing from one town to the other if it weren't for the city limits sign.

This tour begins on Victory Drive at the foot of the Thunderbolt Bridge across the Wilmington River. For a brief, scenic excursion along the river, turn right off Victory Drive onto River Road. Follow River Road for 0.6 mile along a knoll overlooking the river. Often, you can see the local shrimp fleet tied at the docks along the water. The views of the river, the surrounding marshes, and the huge, moss-draped oaks lining River Road are images you will not soon forget.

River Road in Thunderbolt

According to a legend passed down directly from the mouth of James Oglethorpe, Thunderbolt received its name when a bolt of lightning struck the ground and shattered the underlying rock, opening up a spring. Supposedly, the burning smell caused by the thunderbolt lingered at the spring for many years afterward.

Oglethorpe considered Thunderbolt to be of strategic importance. He ordered a settlement and fort built here, the first of three such projects designed to protect the water approaches to Savannah from incursions by the Spanish; the other fortified settlements were on Skidaway and Tybee islands.

By 1734, Thunderbolt boasted a hexagonal palisade, earthen breastworks, a battery of four cannons, and ten resident families. Those families stayed hard at work raising hogs, cattle, and poultry, growing gardens, making potash, and cultivating raw silk. Soon, Thunderbolt was serving as a point of embarkation for Frederica and points south.

Thunderbolt played a major role in the siege of Savannah during the Revolutionary War. Charles-Henri, Comte d'Estaing, the leader of the French forces sent to help the Americans, set up his base of operations at Thunderbolt. He took possession of a large, beautiful home, which was subsequently used as both a hospital and as the place from which signals were sent to ships offshore.

In 1856, an attempt was made to change the town's name to Warsaw. Custom and public opinion held sway, however, and the local citizens declined to go along with the official change. The name Thunderbolt remained in popular use. In 1921, the town was finally incorporated under that name.

In 1875, a casino was built in Thunderbolt on land bordering the river. It proved one of the most popular recreational spots in the Savannah area, with fortune seekers coming by streetcar, road, and water. On November 2, 1930, the casino went up in a spectacular blaze. The Thunderbolt Marina was built on its former site.

Today, Thunderbolt is known mostly for its location on the Wilmington River, which doubles as the Intracoastal Waterway in this area.

When you have fully enjoyed the scenery along the river, retrace your route to Victory Drive. There is a fork in the road immediately on the other side of Victory Drive. Cross Victory and take the left fork to continue on River Road; after two blocks, the name changes to Bonaventure Road. It is 0.7 mile from Victory Drive to a stop sign at a three-way intersection. Turn right onto the grounds of Bonaventure Cemetery. The brick building on the right is the cemetery office. After entering the gates, bear right. Just ahead on the left are signs directing you to the historic section.

The lovely tract of land that is Bonaventure Cemetery was settled around 1760 by an English colonel named John Mulryne. He named his plantation from the Italian words *buono ventura*, or "good fortune." True to its name, it was a place of great beauty, one of the choicest sites in the Savannah area. Mulryne constructed a brick house facing his terraced garden.

When Josiah Tattnall of Charleston, South Carolina, married Mulryne's daughter Mary in 1761, the wedding was a brilliant event in the annals of Savannah society. In honor of the union, Mulryne ordered avenues of live oaks planted on the Bonaventure grounds so as to form the letters *M* and *T*. Those oaks may still be seen throughout the cemetery today.

One night during the years that followed, a lively dinner party was in progress at the manor house at Bonaventure when the roof caught fire. When it was decided that the house could not be saved, the gracious hosts suggested that the dinner be removed to the oak trees, where it was carried off with hardly a hitch.

The Revolutionary War was a stressful time around Savannah. In 1778, Josiah Tattnall, a Tory, refused a commission in the British army, yet would not fight against England either. He was shunned by the local patriots, and the Bonaventure estate, though still technically the property of the Mulryne family, was confiscated. Tattnall and his two sons, John and Josiah Jr., departed for England.

John Tattnall, who sided with his father, became a lieutenant in the King's Rangers. But Josiah Jr., only twelve, protested earnestly against leaving his birthplace. When he turned eighteen, he returned to Georgia, where he sought out General Nathanael Greene's army and offered his services. He so distinguished himself with his patriotism that the state eventually let him buy back Bonaventure, his grandparents' estate. He lived there for eighteen years. He later became a member of the state legislature, a member of Congress, and governor of Georgia.

Josiah Tattnall, Jr., died in 1804 at the age of thirty-eight. His death came in the West Indies, where he had gone seeking to recover his health. During his life, he had frequently expressed a desire to be buried beneath the oaks at Bonaventure, where he had played as a child. His wife was already buried there, and according to his wishes, he was sent home to join her.

Josiah Jr. left an orphaned son, Josiah Tattnall III. Custody fell to the boy's grandfather, the original Josiah Tattnall chased out of America during the Revolution. He brought the young boy to England to be educated. Six years later, Josiah III returned to America and joined the navy.

Bonaventure Cemetery

Like his forbears, Josiah III struggled with his allegiance to the United States and England. On one occasion, he deserted the American navy to come to the aid of the British fleet, which was fighting in Chinese waters, an act that drew international attention. When he was reprimanded for breaching America's neutrality, Josiah III simply replied, "Blood is thicker than water." His remark played well in England, and actually helped bring about the first positive feelings between the two countries since the War of 1812.

The distinguished military career of Josiah Tattnall III lasted all the way to the Civil War, when he served as a commodore for the Confederates.

In 1850, Captain Peter Wiltberger, owner of the Pulaski Hotel, purchased Bonaventure and turned it into a cemetery. It was called the Evergreen Cemetery of Bonaventure until July 1907, when the property passed into the ownership of the city of Savannah and was placed under the jurisdiction of the Park and Tree Commission. Since then, it has been known as Bonaventure Cemetery.

The remains of Josiah Tattnall III lie in Section E of the cemetery, along with those of his parents and several Tattnall children who died in infancy. Nearby, in Section D, are the graves of Noble Jones and his son Noble Wimberly Jones. (For information about Noble Jones and his descendants, see The Wormsloe Tour, pages 75–78.)

Noble Jones marker
at Bonaventure Cemetery

The graveyard hosted a famous visitor in 1867. A young Scotsman named John Muir had left Louisville, Kentucky, intending to walk to the tip of mainland Florida, a distance of 1,000 miles. When he reached Savannah, he was out of money and in need of a place to rest and recuperate. He spent five days camping on the property, where he discovered "one of the most impressive assemblages of animal and plant creatures I have ever met. . . . Never since I was allowed to walk the woods have I found so impressive a company of trees as the tillandsia-draped oaks of Bonaventure."

Muir eventually completed his journey. A gifted explorer, naturalist, writer, and advocate of forest conservation, Muir went on to found the Sierra Club. His efforts influenced Congress to pass the Yosemite National Park Bill in 1890, establishing both Yosemite and Sequoia national parks. He persuaded President Theodore Roosevelt to set aside 148 million acres of forest reserves. A redwood forest in California's Coast Range was named Muir Woods in 1908 to honor his contribution to forest conservation.

After viewing Bonaventure Cemetery, retrace your route to Victory Drive (U.S. 80), turn left, and drive across the Intracoastal Waterway. Proceed 2.8 miles to the intersection with Islands Expressway. Turn left onto the expressway and continue 1.8 miles to another bridge across the Wilmington River. Along this route, you will see large homes facing the river, with boats riding at anchor at their docks. You will also see vast marsh areas and pine forests. Continue for 1.2 miles after the bridge through a coastal landscape of myrtle and palmetto. Turn right at the signs directing you to Old Fort Jackson Historic Site.

Fort Jackson is Georgia's oldest standing military fortification. During the Revolutionary War, patriot forces erected a battery on the grounds of a former brickyard at the present site of Fort Jackson. An outbreak of malaria led to the evacuation of the battery before it ever fired a shot.

But this location was too strategic to abandon for long. All boats coming into Savannah's harbor had to pass this site. The marshes surrounding the area offered protection from land attack, and deep anchorage near the shoreline allowed easy shipment of supplies and troops.

Fort Jackson

In 1808, President Thomas Jefferson proposed a national system of forts to guard America's coast. At the time, war with either France or Britain seemed imminent. Captain William McRee, who had graduated from West Point in 1805 while still a teenager, was sent to design and supervise the construction of a fort at this location. A brick battery, a wooden barracks, and a powder magazine were completed before war with Britain began in 1812.

After the War of 1812, further construction at the fort saw the addition of the moat and drawbridge, more barracks, privies, a rear wall, and another powder magazine.

During the Civil War, Fort Jackson became the Confederate headquarters for the Savannah River defenses. The Confederate presence at Fort Jackson prevented Savannah from suffering a sea attack.

The commander of the forces here was Edward Clifford Anderson. Prior to the war, Anderson had served several terms as mayor of Savannah. In fact, despite being on the losing side, he later became Savannah's first postwar mayor as well.

In November 1861, Anderson ran the Union blockade of Savannah with the largest single shipment of war supplies the Confederacy would ever receive through the blockade. When Savannah fell to Sherman's forces at the end of his "March to the Sea," Anderson and his forces crossed the river into South Carolina and eluded capture.

Today, the fort is maintained by the Coastal Heritage Society. Its museum is housed in the actual rooms of the inner fort, and a self-guided tour is available. Fort Jackson is a fine place to spend time enjoying the scenery, talking with the friendly people who work there, and soaking up the history of the area. One piece of advice is in order, however: bring insect repellent to keep the giant mosquitoes at bay. As John Roberson, an employee at the fort, said, "They are so big you can see the stripes on their legs. They are so big they are called 'Tiger Mosquitoes.'"

Fort Jackson

Return to Islands Expressway, turn left, and retrace your route to U.S. 80. Turn left, heading east. It is 6.5 miles to a sign directing you to Fort Pulaski National Monument and Coast Guard Station. Along this drive, you will traverse a few islands—Whitemarsh, Talahi, and McQueens—before you cross South Channel onto Cockspur Island, where Fort Pulaski is located. The route, lined with palmettos and oleanders, passes through picturesque tropical foliage and marshes.

Cockspur Island takes its name from the shape of its dangerous reef, which juts out toward the open sound. The island is within sight of the Atlantic Ocean. It guards the two entrances to the Savannah River. Despite the fact that little of the island's acreage lies above the high-water mark, this small piece of land has played an important role in coastal Georgia's history. The island was so strategically important that it was considered the key to the province. Twenty acres on the eastern point were permanently set aside by England as a site for harbor fortifications.

In 1761, Fort George, the first fort here, was constructed in an attempt to provide defense against the Spanish at St. Augustine, Florida. After hostilities with the Spanish died down, the structure was used principally to enforce quarantine and customs regulations.

When the Revolutionary War broke out, the patriots abandoned Fort George when they realized it could not withstand a strong fleet. The fort was barely abandoned when two British warships arrived. With the formidable guns of these warships standing guard, the island became a haven for refugees loyal to the British cause. One such refugee was Sir James Wright, the royal governor, who arrived carrying the great seal of the province. While he resided here, Cockspur Island briefly became the capital of colonial Georgia.

A new fort, Fort Greene, was built in 1794 and 1795 to help safeguard the fledgling republic. Fort Greene did not last long. In September 1804, the island was raked by one of the most violent hurricanes in history. When the storm abated, not a shred of Fort Greene remained.

Plans for a new fort were authorized in 1827, though work didn't actually begin until 1829. This was to be a far more massive undertaking than Forts George and Greene. Early in the construction process, it was discovered that the deep mud of Cockspur Island would not support the proposed structure. The weight of the walls had to be reduced, and heavy wooden piles had to be driven seventy feet into the mud to support the masonry.

In 1833, still relatively early in the construction, it was decided that the fort would be named for Revolutionary War hero Casimir Pulaski. It was fitting.

Pulaski, wounded in the thigh during the Battle of Savannah in October 1779, died two days later and was buried at sea near the mouth of the Savannah River, in the vicinity of Cockspur Island. (For more information about Casimir Pulaski and the Battle of Savannah, see The Lincoln's Christmas Gift Tour, page 29, and The Old Seaport Tour, pages 52–53.)

Work on the fort was finally completed in 1847. It was a stupendous project. Bricks were purchased in lots ranging from 1 to 7 million, with an estimated 25 million in the entire structure. The bricks were made at nearby Hermitage Plantation, as well as in Baltimore, Maryland, and Alexandria, Virginia. Granite from New York and brown sandstone from the Connecticut River Valley were also used.

It is interesting to note that every engineer employed in the construction of the fort became a general in either the Confederate army or the Union army. Among them was a West Point graduate named Robert E. Lee.

A tragic incident occurred at the new fort in October 1855. Unable to settle a family difficulty, John Chaplin of South Carolina, an ex-lieutenant in the United States Navy, and his brother-in-law, a Dr. Kirk of Savannah, met at Fort Pulaski to fight a duel. Three shots were exchanged. According to reports, Chaplin fired the first shot into the air, an attempt at last-minute reconciliation. However, Dr. Kirk refused to respond in kind, but rather fired at Chaplin, slightly wounding him in the foot. In doing so, he forfeited his life, for Chaplin's aim on his second shot proved deadly.

By the time Abraham Lincoln was elected president, only 20 of the planned 146 guns had been mounted at Fort Pulaski. When word reached Savannah that South Carolina had seceded, a garrison of Georgians sympathetic to the Confederate cause took control of the fort.

Charles H. Olmstead, who was appointed colonel, kept a journal of the fort's activities which still serves as an excellent source of information about what happened during this period.

On the morning of April 10, 1862, Colonel Olmstead noted suspicious changes in the landscape of neighboring Tybee Island. The colonel and a lieutenant on duty noticed that several chimneys had been torn down, that the top of the ridge had been leveled, and that dark objects were visible along the ridge. At that moment, a small boat approached Fort Pulaski under a flag of truce. The courier presented a formal demand for surrender. Olmstead answered promptly. His written reply ended, "I am here to defend the Fort, not to surrender it."

A few hours later, a mortar exploded over Fort Pulaski. When a second shell fell short, the Confederates believed they had little to fear from the Union guns. They had little way of knowing that the Union troops were using new rifled cannons. This was the first time guns of this design were used in warfare.

The next morning, the Union guns fired again. This time, they were accurate. By noon, the guns on the ramparts of Fort Pulaski were silenced, and the fort sported two gaping holes in its walls. Olmstead realized that surrender was inevitable. When he presented his sword to Captain Quincy A. Gillmore of the Union forces, he remarked, "I yield my sword, but I trust I have not disgraced it."

Today, visitors can tour Fort Pulaski and get an idea of what the fortifications were like during the Civil War. The entire fort is surrounded by a moat seven feet deep and ranging from thirty-two to forty-eight feet in width. On the rear, or west, wall, a drawbridge and a heavily fortified entrance give access to the fort. The winches and counterweights that were used to raise the drawbridge are visible in the rooms on either side of the entrance. As the drawbridge was raised, a strong, wooden grille was lowered into place behind it, and bolt-studded doors were closed behind that. Just in case enemy forces penetrated that far, they then had to walk a gauntlet between two rows of rifle slits and through another set of doors before gaining access to the interior of

Entrance to Fort Pulaski

Fort Pulaski moat

Fort Pulaski

the fort. The defenses throughout the rest of Fort Pulaski are equally impressive. All the same, the fort fell to Union bombardment within thirty hours. Some of the damage has been left unrepaired to show the fury of the attack. Many of the 5,275 Union shots are still visible in the exterior walls.

Fort Pulaski offers a nice family outing, especially for anyone interested in military history. While strolling the grounds, be sure to visit the John Wesley Memorial, located north of the parking lot and the entrance to the fort.

When James Oglethorpe came to America to establish the Georgia colony, his immediate concerns were providing adequate defense and a means of basic sustenance for the settlers. However, he also recognized that the colonists had spiritual needs, and that it would take a preacher with a great deal of energy to minister to a province that was 200 miles long.

When Oglethorpe returned to England for a visit in 1735, he asked John Wesley, the future founder of the Methodist faith, to come to Georgia with him. Wesley initially declined, but under pressure from his mother, Oglethorpe, and a member of the colony's board of trustees, he finally agreed. His brother, Charles, accompanied him to the New World. (For more information about Charles Wesley, see The Marshes of Glynn Tour, pages 135–36.)

Unfortunately, there was a misunderstanding at the root of John Wesley's acceptance of the post. Oglethorpe and the trustees wanted him to minister strictly to the colonists. But Wesley understood that he was going to Georgia to preach to the Indians, a far more romantic calling, and one that appealed to his sense of adventure.

Wesley landed on Cockspur Island on February 5, 1736. Initially, his ministry in Georgia showed promise. He was welcomed not only by the British colonists, but by Spaniards, Germans, and Jews in the area as well. On one occasion, two separate events—a ball and a prayer meeting conducted by Wesley—were to be held simultaneously in Savannah. The story goes that Wesley's church was packed, but that the ballroom was so deserted that the entertainment had to be canceled.

Soon, things began to deteriorate. Wesley continually expressed his desire to go among the Indians, while Oglethorpe just as frequently cautioned him to remain among the settlers. On the occasions when Wesley did talk with the Indians, he found them wholly unreceptive to his preaching, or too wrapped up in warfare to even listen to him. This came as a major disappointment, and Wesley's opinions turned extremely dark. He characterized the Indians as "gluttons, drunkards, thieves, dissemblers, liars" who were "implacable, unmerciful; murderers of fathers, murderers of mothers, murderers of their own children." The Indians, he wrote, showed "no inclination to learn any thing, but least of all Christianity."

Wesley fell from grace with the settlers as well. He had been cautioned by the trustees to be tolerant of colonists with widely different religious backgrounds, but shortly after his arrival, he began showing an authoritarian streak that did not sit well with the people of Georgia. For example, he insisted upon baptism by immersion unless an infant was too weak to be "dipped." On one occasion, when a woman expressed her preference that her healthy infant be merely sprinkled with water, he declined to perform the rite.

But the incident that ended Wesley's stay in America was a love affair that turned bitter. Among his converts to Christianity was an attractive, engaging girl named Sophia Hopkins. The young minister fell for her. Their relationship progressed to a point where a marriage proposal seemed imminent, at which time Wesley began hesitating between his commitment to his Christian mission and his love. Feeling she was being spurned, Sophia quickly accepted a marriage proposal from another suitor, William Williamson. Unable to let go, Wesley tried to get her to attend church functions against her wishes and spoke harshly to her on a public street. Ultimately, he refused to serve her communion one Sunday in church. He was promptly served with a warrant for defaming Sophia's character, with William Williamson suing him for 1,000 pounds in damages. Though Wesley was reluctant to recognize civil authority in what he considered a religious matter, he showed up in court on the appointed date. Williamson didn't, and the suit never came to pass.

John Wesley's career in Georgia was over. He returned to England after less than two years on American soil. It was a rare dark period in what was to be an outstanding life of Christian service.

When you have fully enjoyed Fort Pulaski, retrace your route to U.S. 80 and turn left, heading east. After crossing Lazaretto Creek 0.9 mile later, you will be on Tybee Island.

A lazaretto is a hospital that cares for people with contagious diseases. Constructed in 1767, the lazaretto on Tybee Island initially served as a quarantine station. Later, it was converted to a slave hospital, where traders left their sick slaves. If the slaves recovered, they were sold in the slave market in Savannah. If they died, they were buried in unmarked graves on Tybee Island. The lazaretto that once stood on the west end of the island no longer exists, but Lazaretto Creek preserves its memory.

Continue 2.1 miles to the sign reading "Historic Tybee Lighthouse and Museum." Turn left on Campbell Avenue and drive two blocks. Turn left on

Van Horne Street and continue one block to Meddin Drive. Turn right on Meddin and you will see the lighthouse.

Tybee Island guards the southern flank of the Savannah River's outlet to the sea. The original township of Tybee was founded by James Oglethorpe in 1733. After the more urgent needs of the settlers were cared for, Oglethorpe ordered the construction of a beacon on the inlet where a creek separated Tybee and Skidaway islands.

Oglethorpe selected William Blithemann as the master carpenter and sent as many men as could be spared. They worked for two shillings a day in the construction of the lighthouse. The beacon was prefabricated in Savannah and carried down to Tybee to be assembled. The work progressed nicely, and Oglethorpe predicted that the construction would be finished by March 1734.

All who saw the lighthouse under construction marveled at it. One observer described it as "a Tower of Wood of a prodigious Height." Octagonal in shape, upon completion it would stand 90 feet high and have a width of 25 feet at the bottom and 12.5 feet at the top. Weatherboarding would cover the sides to a height of 26 feet, with the remainder left open.

To expedite construction, Oglethorpe settled ten families on the island, granting each a fifty-acre lot. Although it seemed pleasant enough to the casual visitor, the island was not a healthy place to live. William Stephens, the appointed representative of the trustees of the Georgia colony at that time, later described Tybee Island as "a Place so exceedingly pestered with Musketoes, by Reason of the adjacent Marshes, that no Person would ever be fond of taking his Abode there."

Several settlers died during the construction. At the time, no one thought to attribute it to the mosquitoes. In fact, many Savannah residents thought the settlers died from drinking too much rum.

It soon became necessary to transport workmen from Savannah. More families were moved onto the island to supply labor.

When Oglethorpe returned to the colony in early 1736 after a visit to England, he was so angered by the slow progress on the lighthouse that he imprisoned the master carpenter and threatened to hang him. The laborers intervened to save the master carpenter, promising to complete the structure within five weeks. In the next sixteen days, more work was done than in the preceding sixteen months.

The lighthouse was completed in the spring of 1736, two years behind Oglethorpe's schedule. By September 1737, the island was deserted. During their years on the island, the settlers had begun only two huts and a house, completing none of the three. Tybee Island was once again the property of the opossums, raccoons, and other animal inhabitants.

During the entire time the first beacon stood at Tybee, no pilot was stationed there to care for it. In 1739, Peter Emery, a man who knew the local waters well, applied for the position of pilot to help guide ships through the treacherous channels. But because of several delays in approving his appointment, Emery finally announced the he "would not be confined to live at Tybee on any Terms."

Tybee Lighthouse

The winter of 1740–41 was especially fierce. The lighthouse was damaged by severe storms. Noble Jones and Thomas Sumner, a master carpenter living at Frederica, were sent to inspect it. At first, they thought the lighthouse could be repaired, but it wasn't long before another storm shook it so badly that several main timbers broke. It leaned so precariously that Sumner wrote that it was "dangerous to go near it, much more to touch it with a Tool."

The lighthouse finally collapsed in a storm in August 1741. By then, coastal citizens were fed up with the entire project. A Charleston newspaper, the *South Carolina Gazette*, saw fit to use the lighthouse to criticize officials in the fledgling colony to the south:

> This fine Piece of Workmanship, so beneficial to all those who fall in with the Coast of South-Carolina and Georgia, was erected at the beginning of the year 1736. . . . It's Fall is entirely owing to the want of Covering; the Frame being expos'd was quite rotted. This was many times represented to the ruling Powers in Georgia, but to no Purpose, altho they were told it could have been Weather-boarded for 100 Pounds Sterling, which in all probability would have made it stand for Twenty or Thirty Years longer—What better can be expected from those who Regard their own Passions and private Interest more than the good of their Country and Fellow Subjects.

A new beacon was begun, this time with Thomas Sumner in charge of construction. Timbers were sawed at Thunderbolt and floated to Tybee Island on rafts.

The second lighthouse was completed in March 1742. William Stephens, the trustees' representative, described it as "a piece of work, of such strength and Beauty, tho plain." Oglethorpe claimed it was "much the best building of that kind in America." He thought so highly of it that he considered "casting up a Retrenchment round it, with a little Fortification, to defend it from any suddain [*sic*] or secret attack." That was later accomplished, though not during Oglethorpe's day.

Oglethorpe praised Sumner highly to the trustees. Sumner just happened to be in London at the time. Taking advantage of the opportunity presented him, he petitioned for and was granted five hundred acres of land near Frederica. He was also given permission to carry six indentured servants back to Georgia for a period of five years. This grant helped to make Sumner a prosperous man.

Over the years, the lighthouse saw frequent repairs. It was entirely rebuilt in 1757 and replaced in 1773.

Finally, in 1781, a masonry lighthouse was constructed on roughly the same spot as its wooden predecessors. The tower was fitted with a new, smokeless, hollow-wick oil lamp that allowed air to flow around and through the wick, thus creating a brighter light than simple candles. When President George Washington was sent a proposal for a staircase for the lighthouse, he was given two options: a hanging staircase costing 160 pounds, or a plain staircase costing 110 pounds. Washington, in his typical frugal fashion, wrote, "Approved with the plain staircase. G. Washington."

During the Civil War, retreating Confederate forces attempted to blow up the lighthouse by detonating a keg of gunpowder inside the tower. The light was extinguished, but the brick shell survived, and the beacon was relit in 1867.

Tybee Lighthouse

As part of its postwar restoration, the lighthouse was raised to a height of 144 feet at the focal point of the light and 154 feet at its highest point. The bottom half was painted white, the upper half black. A first-order Fresnel lens was installed; it remains in place today. The light from the tower can be seen 20 miles out to sea under ideal conditions.

Storms in 1871 and 1878 and an earthquake in 1886 left cracks in the tower wall.

Plans to rebuild the tower have never been implemented, so you will find the light much as it was after the Civil War.

Another interesting structure on Tybee is Fort Screven, which guards the northern shore of the island and overlooks the southern flank of the Savannah River's inlet.

In 1786, the Georgia legislature passed a law providing for a fort on either Cockspur Island or Tybee Island. The legislature ordered that the fort be named in honor of General James Screven, a Georgia native who lost his life in Liberty County, just to the south, during the Revolutionary War.

The fort was a long time in coming. The property on Tybee Island came under federal control in 1875. Construction of the fort began in 1897. The first battery was completed in 1898 and the entire fort in 1905. It remained in active use as the Fort Screven Reservation until 1945. It was used as a coastal artillery fort, an infantry post, and a school for deep-sea diving. Among the many distinguished officers who saw duty here was George C. Marshall, who served as the commanding colonel at one time. When Fort Screven was declared surplus, it was acquired by the town of Tybee.

Over the years, Tybee Island has attracted people other than military men and lighthouse keepers. From 1820 to 1860, the island earned a reputation as a dueling site. Gentlemen from South Carolina frequently rowed across the river to duel in this remote place. South Carolinians were not prosecuted for dueling in the state of Georgia, so this proved a convenient place to defend their honor and settle disputes.

Also in the nineteenth century, Tybee Island became a popular recreational area. In the beginning, it was only accessible by sailboat or steamer, but in 1887, a railroad was built from Savannah to the island. The railroad allowed Savannah residents to escape for the day, their picnic baskets jammed with fried chicken, pound cake, and other foods.

And thanks to the Fresh Air Home, Tybee Island has long been a haven for children. Opened in 1898 with a budget of $100 for rent and operating expenses, the Fresh Air Home was originally a convalescent home for children with respiratory and other physical problems. Over the years, it has expanded in both scope and size. Today, it serves as a summer vacation spot for city youths, accommodating approximately a hundred children every two weeks. For many years, the home has prided itself on its nourishing meals. During one two-week period in 1950, it was noted that 250 more pounds of children left the Fresh Air Home than had arrived there.

Today, easy access to the island's beaches has led to heavy residential development. Tybee remains a popular resort area.

This tour ends at the lighthouse and the Tybee Museum, both of which are contained within the walls of Fort Screven. You can tour the Tybee Museum, with its gun collection, its doll collection, and its exhibits on the history of Tybee Island and Fort Screven; you can climb the lighthouse for a wonderful view of the ocean; or you can simply spend an enjoyable day on the beach.

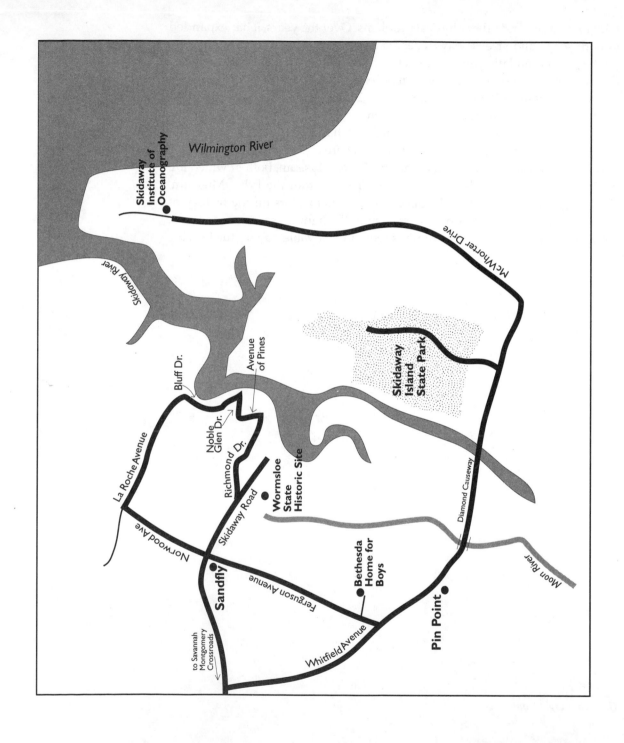

The Wormsloe Tour

This tour covers Wormsloe State Historic Site, the Isle of Hope Historic District, and the former site of Sandfly. It continues to the Bethesda Home for Boys, Pin Point, and the Skidaway Institute of Oceanography.

Total mileage: approximately 14 miles.

This tour begins at Wormsloe State Historic Site. The former plantation is located 8 miles southeast of Savannah at 7601 Skidaway Road. If you are traveling on I-95, take Exit 16 and proceed east toward Savannah on GA 204 (Abercorn Street). It is 10.3 miles on GA 204 to Montgomery Crossroads. Turn right and drive 3.2 miles until the road ends at Skidaway Road. Turn right and proceed 0.8 mile to the entrance of the historic site.

The impressive gate at Wormsloe State Historic Site marks the entrance to a 1.5-mile-long avenue of live oaks. These oaks were planted in the early 1890s to commemorate the birth of Wymberley Wormsloe DeRenne; the gate was erected in 1913 to celebrate his coming of age. Beyond the avenue are traces of an Old South plantation that is a "must see" for visitors.

The first fortified house at what was then called Wormslow was built between 1739 and 1745 by Noble Jones, one of the colonists who accompanied General James Oglethorpe to Georgia in 1733. When Oglethorpe brought the first Georgia colonists to America, the trustees of the colony envisioned the silk culture as one of the primary sources of income for the settlers. But after a few years, the colonists petitioned the trustees to turn funds toward other means of agriculture and commerce. Two of the reasons the silk culture never really caught on in the colony were early fires at the silk warehouses and the worms' dislike for the mulberry leaves grown in Georgia, a different kind from those in Europe.

The trustees, however, were not deterred from their original plan. They even offered large bounties to those who would engage in the growth of silk. One of the colonists who decided to take advantage of the bounty was Noble Jones. A native of Lambeth, England, on the south bank of the Thames River, Jones came to the New World with his wife, Sarah, his daughter, Mary, and his son, Noble Wimberly Jones. He practiced medicine in the colony.

In 1736, Jones requested a lease for property on the Isle of Hope, 10 miles from Savannah. He may have named his property Wormslow in honor of the silkworms he planned to cultivate. A more popular belief is that, like a number of settlers, he wanted to give a Welsh touch to his new surroundings; Wormslow is Welsh for "dragon's lair." Along with the mulberry trees needed for silk production, Jones grew rice and cotton and raised cattle.

Although his house was rather plain and consisted of only five rooms, it was built on a grand scale. Jones used a substance known as tabby for his building material. The ingredients in tabby—oyster shells, lime, sand, and water—were all plentiful in the area. The practice of building structures of tabby probably came from the Spanish, though some date it to Roman times. As early as 1509, Ponce de Leon's house in Puerto Rico was built of *tapia*, a name later anglicized to tabby. By the time Jones began his home, tabby was a standard building material in semitropical climates because of its durability.

The greatest threat to the original Georgia colonists was the Spanish settlement at St. Augustine, Florida. As early as 1739, a small fort was established on Jones's property. In 1740, Oglethorpe led a brief expedition against the Spanish, with Jones serving as a lieutenant. Upon their return, they feared a reprisal. A company of marines was quartered in huts near Jones's home at Wormslow and assigned to watch the inlets to guard against a surprise attack.

Entrance to
Wormsloe State Historic Site

TOURING THE COASTAL GEORGIA BACKROADS

Noble Jones dabbled in plant experimentation. One of his experiments, the century plant, a twenty-four-foot blooming plant, became a local attraction in 1756. It was featured in a Savannah newspaper.

In fact, Wormslow became so well known for its plant experiments that John and William Bartram, famed naturalists, visited the plantation in 1765. John Bartram, born in Pennsylvania in 1699, planted the first botanical garden on American soil. He helped Benjamin Franklin found the American Philosophical Society. His son William, born near Philadelphia in 1739, was one of the first notable American ornithologists. His book *Travels*, published in 1791, tells of the years he spent exploring Florida, Georgia, and the Carolinas; the book is so rich in colorful detail that Samuel Coleridge and William Wordsworth used it as a source for some of their poems.

John Bartram was impressed by Wormslow. In his journal, he described it as a plantation where unusual fruits such as pomegranates, oranges, figs, peaches, and apricots were grown.

Noble Jones was active in the royal province after it established its independence from the trustees. He was offered a seat on the coveted Governor's Council. But when cries for independence from England arose, Jones remained loyal to his homeland. He died in 1775, before the Revolutionary War began. Noble Jones was probably the last surviving head of the original families who arrived with James Oglethorpe aboard the *Anne*.

His son, Noble Wimberly Jones, had come to the New World with his parents at the age of ten. Like so many young men who had done most of their growing up on American soil, he sided with the patriots. In fact, he was so active in the patriot cause that he was forced to flee Savannah when the British gained control of that city in 1778. When the British captured Charleston, Noble Wimberly Jones was taken captive. He was released on parole the following year and returned to Savannah, where he practiced medicine until his death in 1805.

George Jones was the only one of Noble Wimberly Jones's fourteen children who survived him. It was George Jones who, through his knowledgeable business dealings and his three judicious marriages, solidified the family fortune. He died in 1838.

The following year, the family began construction on a mansion in exclusive Newport, Rhode Island, so as to spend summers away from the humidity and the mosquito-carried diseases of the low-lying rice fields; that mansion, called Kingscote, still exists today. When the Civil War was imminent, the Jones family transported its furniture and books, the inventory of its wine cellar, and even its gold-trimmed French porcelain dinner service for twenty-four from the Newport residence. The shipment reached Savannah aboard the last boat to arrive before the blockade was enforced. The furniture and five barrels of porcelain spent the war in a warehouse before finally being transferred to the Jones heirs after the conflict.

George Frederick Tilghman Jones was the son of George Jones. Around the time of the Civil War, there happened to be another prominent man by the name of George Jones in Savannah, and both he and George Frederick Tilghman Jones grew frustrated with the constant confusion of names. George Frederick Tilghman Jones solved the problem by changing the family name to DeRenne, an improvisation on his grandmother's name, Van Deren. Thereafter, he signed himself George Wymberley Jones DeRenne. He was also the man who changed the spelling of the estate's name to Wormsloe.

Over the generations, the Jones/DeRenne men grew less interested in public service and more concerned with literary pursuits, amassing great collections of rare books and doing a little writing and publishing as well. When he died in 1880, George Wymberley Jones DeRenne left both a literary legacy and the richest estate in Savannah, appraised at $700,377.06.

Today, Jones descendants still retain 65.5 acres near the avenue of live oak trees. As you drive through the gate and down the avenue of oaks, you will see the family's gracious white clapboard house in the trees on the left. This house dates to 1828; it is not open to the public.

The Georgia Department of Natural Resources operates the remaining 822 acres of the property as the Wormsloe State Historic Site. Past the Jones home, you will come to a parking lot at the museum. For the price of admission, you can enjoy the museum, a movie on the life and times of Noble Jones, and a trail system leading back to the river.

Be sure to walk the trail leading under magnificent old trees to the tabby ruins of the Noble Jones manor house. This home was never known for its magnificence, though you will get some idea of its size and sturdiness from the tabby foundation. An old cemetery is nearby. Noble Jones and most of his family were interred at Bonaventure Cemetery (see The Tybee Light Tour, page 60), but it is believed that his wife, Sarah, and his son Inigo were buried here. The trail continues to the Skidaway River, where you can view huge marshes, large stands of cedar trees, and white yachts in the distance.

Visitors sometimes wonder why coastal Georgia has fewer and, as in the case of the old estate of Noble Jones, less grand plantation homes than neighboring South Carolina.

Tabby ruins at Wormsloe

Avenue of oaks at Wormsloe

Two of the most often-used explanations—that prohibitions against slavery led to fewer and smaller estates in Georgia and that Sherman destroyed a great many plantation homes on his "March to the Sea"—simply don't hold water. It is true that the trustees initially barred slavery in Georgia because they felt it would weaken the colony's military strength and lessen the industrious spirit of the colonists. However, such idealism proved short-lived, as slavery was instituted in Georgia within sixteen years of the colony's founding. And as for Sherman, he placed his men under orders not to loot or otherwise damage property when he reached Savannah. His men actually did little damage along the immediate Georgia coastline.

The primary reason that South Carolina has more plantations than Georgia is simply that South Carolina is older. Actually, Georgia does have its fair share of plantation estates. Some have been lost to fire over the years, others along the Savannah River have been lost to industrialization, and still others are privately owned and not open to the public.

When you leave the entrance to Wormsloe State Historic Site, turn right on Skidaway Road. Continue 0.2 mile to where Skidaway curves to the left and Richmond Drive, a street divided by a row of moss-draped oak trees, continues straight ahead. Follow Richmond Drive for 0.5 mile to where it ends. Turn left onto Avenue of Pines and continue 0.2 mile to Noble Glen Drive.

Turn right to enter the Isle of Hope Historic District. At the end of Noble Glen Drive, turn left onto Bluff Drive, which runs along the Skidaway River.

Tucked away on the Isle of Hope are some of the choicest parcels of real estate in the Southeast. On the left are well-proportioned homes with high-pitched roofs and window boxes. On the right are docks and boathouses that jut into the river. Huge trees in the yards reach out over the road.

After traveling 0.6 mile on Bluff Drive, turn left onto LaRoche Avenue. Continue 1.1 miles to Norwood Avenue. Turn left again. Follow the palm-lined Norwood Avenue for 1 mile. If you have a sweet tooth, you may want to make a quick stop at the Byrd Cookie Company, located on the left at 2233 Norwood; this is a favorite spot for visitors and locals alike. It is another 0.1 mile to the intersection with Skidaway Road, where Norwood Avenue changes to Ferguson Avenue.

This intersection was once the site of the community of Sandfly, whose residents combined a strong belief in hexes, spells, spirits, hags, and the like with regular churchgoing and the singing of spirituals. One prominent local resident was Madam Truth, who was famous for her seances, during which her voice would become lower-pitched, her hands would move involuntarily, and her eyes would roll back in her head. Though the people of Sandfly were half-terrified of her, they came to her whenever they desired to know the outcome of a business venture or the direction a courtship was taking. For her part, Madam Truth always insisted that those who patronized her be baptized at the Holy Sanctified Church of Sandfly.

Continue 2.2 miles on Ferguson Avenue to the Bethesda Home for Boys, one of the most historic sites in the Savannah area. The entrance to the orphanage resembles a plantation entrance. The imposing brick-columned entry leads into an avenue of oaks. On the left is an immense pasture where dozens of white-faced cattle graze.

The founders of Georgia intended it to be a colony that would offer a second chance to convicts who had fallen into debt during difficult economic times; however, as it turned out, very few, if any, of the original Georgia settlers were debtors.

So, too, was the founding of Bethesda grounded in humanitarian concerns. In the early years, the mortality rate in the colony was quite high, with the result that many children were orphaned. Though these children were generally taken in by other families, the motive was more often to put them to hard work rather than to raise them in a nurturing environment. James Oglethorpe found this state of affairs unacceptable, and John Wesley agreed

Entrance gate for
Bethesda Home for Boys

TOURING THE COASTAL GEORGIA BACKROADS

with him. (For information about John Wesley in Georgia, see The Tybee Light Tour, pages 67–68.)

In 1736, Wesley asked a friend and fellow minister, George Whitefield, to come from England and establish an orphanage in Georgia. Whitefield agreed to come to Georgia to assess the need for such a facility. He brought with him a friend and schoolmaster, James Habersham, who would help oversee the project if it was in fact needed.

It didn't take Whitefield long to reach a conclusion. He later wrote, "The poor little ones were tabled out here and there, and besides the hurt they received by bad examples, forgot at home what they learned at school. Others were at hard service and likely to have no education at all. Upon seeing this I thought I could not better show my regard to God and my country than by getting a house and land for these children where they might learn to labor, read and write, and at the same time be brought up in the nurture and admonition of the Lord."

Whitefield was a tireless worker, a powerful preacher, and one of the most well-known men of his day. He quickly won the support of the people of Georgia. So began a thirty-two-year career centered around raising funds for Bethesda that would see him cross the Atlantic thirteen times and preach an estimated eighteen thousand sermons, which averages out to five hundred per year, or ten per week. Whitefield was so convincing that he even managed to charm the notoriously tight-fisted Benjamin Franklin during one of his fund-raising trips to the North. As Franklin put it in his autobiography,

> I happened . . . to attend one of his sermons, in the course of which I perceived that he intended to finish with a collection, and I silently resolved that he should get nothing from me. I had in my pocket a handful of coppermoney, three or four silver dollars, and five pistoles in gold. As he proceeded I began to soften and concluded to give the coppers. Another stroke of his oratory made me ashamed of that and determined me to give the silver, and he finished so admirably that I emptied my pocket into the collector's dish, gold and all.

James Habersham was the administrator of Bethesda. He also oversaw preaching duties in the Savannah area during Whitefield's frequent fund-raising absences. A capable educator, Habersham found less success when he tried braving the long shadow cast by Whitefield's pulpit. As William Stephens, the president of the Georgia colony, noted in his journal in October

1740, "Mr. Habersham read the Church-Service, and Sermons, Morning and Afternoon: wherein he was so fond of aping the Gestures and Manner of some of our late Teachers, that even reading the Lessons out of the Bible, whether historical, or not, he affected a vehement Emphasis, frequently in the wrong Place too; and turning himself to and fro in several Postures towards different Parts of the Congregation, many People looked upon it as ridiculous, instead of giving reverened [sic] Attention to God's Word."

Work toward establishing Bethesda, which means "house of mercy," proceeded quickly. Whitefield sailed to England to petition for a land grant for the orphanage; in early 1739, the trustees granted 500 acres. When news of Whitefield's success reached Georgia, Habersham petitioned James Oglethorpe to assign the orphanage a tract, which proved to be the current property 15 miles south of Savannah, opposite the land of Noble Jones.

In January 1739, officials began collecting orphans for the proposed home. By the time Whitefield returned to the New World, Habersham had already stocked the property with cattle and poultry and begun constructing the original buildings. Work on the main house began in March.

That is not to say there weren't a few problems along the way. With his headstrong ways, Habersham had several clashes with officials of the colony. A load of bricks headed for Bethesda was stolen by privateers. And some families objected when they learned that working-age orphans living in their

Bethesda Home for Boys

homes were to be sent to Bethesda for their education.

All the same, the orphanage's buildings were in place by November 1740, and the original group of sixty-one residents was taken from Savannah to Bethesda over what some say was the first road constructed anywhere in Georgia, though that has never been verified. Among the cosmopolitan group were twenty-three children of English descent, ten Scotch, four Dutch, five French, and seven "Americans."

Bethesda Home for Boys

Even before that, Habersham had begun taking in students who were not orphans in Bethesda's temporary quarters in Savannah. In December 1740, just after the move to the permanent location, Habersham announced his surprise marriage to one such student, a sixteen-year-old girl named Mary Bolton. Her father, Robert Bolton, had heard Whitefield preach in Philadelphia and been so impressed that he sent his daughters, Mary and Rebecca, to Bethesda for their education.

It was the dream of Whitefield and Habersham to make Bethesda self-supporting. All the necessary food was to be grown on the property. Boys were to be taught to be weavers, tailors, and cobblers, while girls were to be taught how to card and spin. All children were to be instructed in silk culture.

This proved difficult to put into practice. Food was scarce at Bethesda in the early years, with the residents having to depend on gifts of deer meat from the Indians and other food from the colonists. Whitefield and Habersham resigned themselves to acquiring outside help, but that didn't work either. Volunteer workers soon grew tired of the menial labor, and indentured servants showed a tendency to escape to South Carolina.

Whitefield and Habersham thus became active in the movement to allow slavery in Georgia. Slaves, they felt, would allow Bethesda to achieve self-sufficiency. To prove the point, Whitefield bought a 640-acre plantation in South Carolina. He named it Providence. By 1748, the eight slaves at Providence had raised buildings and were outproducing the entire work force at Bethesda. The point was made. It was partly due to Whitefield's example that slavery was instituted in Georgia in 1749.

Another dream of Whitefield's, that of transforming Bethesda into a college, came to pass only briefly. He died in 1770, willing the orphanage to his friend Selina Hastings, the countess dowager of Huntington, a distant relative of George Washington; that same year, fire destroyed some buildings at the home, including a section of the main house. Under the countess, Bethesda opened as a college in 1788, but closed upon her death in 1791.

The state took over the property at that time, and the home went into a long downhill slide, the victim of natural disasters and mismanagement. The Savannah Home for Girls was established in 1801. That same year, Bethesda was revived from disrepair, serving only boys this time. In 1805, Bethesda was victimized by another fire and by a hurricane that blew down buildings and salted the school's rice lands. Some of the property had been sold already, and by 1809, affairs were in such a bad state that the state authorized the sale of the rest of the land. The proceeds were divided up among the Savannah poorhouse, the local hospital, Chatham Academy, and the Union Society.

Bethesda's association with the Union Society has proven a most profitable one. Founded in 1750 as the St. George Society, this organization was renamed prior to 1765 in honor of its three known founders, a "union" of a Catholic, a Protestant, and a Jew—Peter Tondee, Richard Milledge, and Benjamin Sheftall. Latter-day members of the Union Society took a deep interest in Bethesda because several of the organization's original members had been raised there. In 1854, the Union Society bought 125 acres of the Bethesda property for $2,500, erected buildings at an expense of $4,700, and moved the children back in.

The Union Society still provides the chief support for Bethesda. Today, Bethesda can lay claim to being the oldest orphanage in America with a continuous existence. And some even claim that the Union Society is the oldest charitable organization in the country.

The arched entrance gate at the orphanage was begun in 1938. Bethesda boys helped in its construction. On the grounds are the beautifully landscaped Lady Huntington Amphitheater and a nonsectarian chapel modeled after George Whitefield's church in England.

Pin Point

Leaving Bethesda, turn left on Ferguson Avenue. After one block, turn left on Diamond Causeway. After 0.6 mile, you will see Pin Point on the right. This small community of muddy driveways, mobile homes, and humble houses, some of which have goats in their yards, is a sharp contrast to the upscale residential developments surrounding it. In 1932, Pin Point was the site of a famous murder, as Limerick "Bo-Cat" De Lancy used an oar to beat and drown his wife, Catherine. Her body, recovered from the water two weeks later, was identifiable only by a corn on one of her toes. This murder was prominent in the local consciousness for many years and was even the subject of a ballad. In more recent years, Pin Point has attained fame as the former home of Supreme Court Justice Clarence Thomas.

After 1.3 more miles on Diamond Causeway, you will cross Moon River, which also serves as the Intracoastal Waterway. Throughout most of its recorded history, Moon River was known as Back River. In 1961, native son Johnny Mercer wrote a song about this beautiful body of water, using the more poetic name "Moon River." In honor of Mercer and his timeless song, the Georgia legislature later made Moon River the official name.

Skidaway Island State Park

After you cross the drawbridge over Moon River and the Intracoastal Waterway, you are on Skidaway Island. Turn left at Skidaway Island Presbyterian Church and continue 0.4 mile on State Park Road to Skidaway Island State Park. This 533-acre park includes campsites, picnic areas, nature walks, a swimming pool, a playground, and beautiful vistas of scenic marshland.

When you are ready to leave the park, return to Diamond Causeway and turn left. Continue 0.4 mile to McWhorter Drive and bear left again. It is 0.4 mile to the Skidaway Institute of Oceanography; McWhorter Drive becomes Modena Island Road at the institute. Turn left at the sign for the Georgia Marine Resources Extension Center. The Skidaway Institute of Oceanography is visible ahead.

The institute sits on a bluff overlooking the Skidaway River. Vessels used for study are anchored at a nearby dock. The Skidaway Institute of Oceanography is the marine-research portion of the University of Georgia. It shares a 680-acre campus with the Georgia Marine Resources Extension Center, which offers an aquarium and exhibits depicting marine and coastal resources. Make sure you tour the aquarium facilities. One of the most popular exhibits shows the evolution of native marine life over a 12,000-year span. The remains of mammoths and extinct whales are among the fossils in the exhibit, as are less exotic specimens like sharks' teeth. The center offers educational programs for all kinds of students, from schoolchildren to serious science and engineering students.

Marine Center

This tour ends at the Skidaway Institute of Oceanography. To return to Savannah, retrace your route on Diamond Causeway, which becomes Whitfield Avenue, then Waters Avenue. Turn left on Montgomery Crossroads. A right on Abercorn Street will then take you to downtown Savannah.

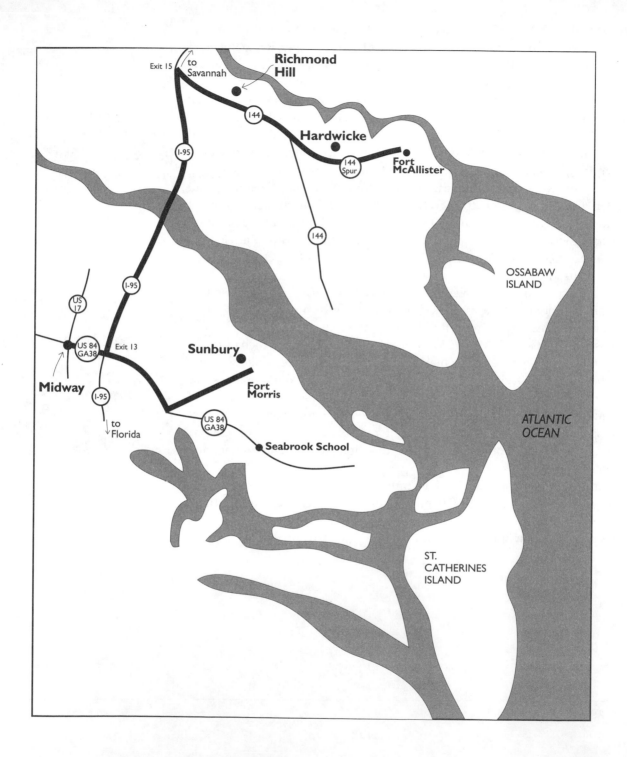

The Signers Tour

This tour begins at the Richmond Hill Fish Hatchery and proceeds through Hardwicke to Fort McAllister. It then continues to Midway Congregational Church. The tour ends at Fort Morris and the former site of Sunbury. From there, you can view the private islands of St. Catherines and Ossabaw.

Total mileage:
approximately 47 miles.

The tour begins at Richmond Hill Fish Hatchery. Leave I-95 at Exit 15 and head east on GA 144. Drive 0.8 mile on this two-lane road to the red brick buildings of the hatchery.

Two of our nation's greatest inventors had an interest in coastal Georgia. The great Thomas Edison once had a laboratory at a power station on the Ogeechee River. And Henry Ford, a great admirer of Edison, subsequently developed ties to the area. After the dissolution of the Hermitage, Henry McAlpin's plantation in Savannah, Ford bought the plantation's manor house and had it moved down the Ogeechee River by barge and reassembled at Richmond Hill. Ford called his 1,700-acre tract on the banks of the river Cherry Hill Plantation. The old Hermitage manor house now stands on private property and cannot be toured.

Many people think of Henry Ford strictly as a manufacturer of automobiles, but his interests ranged from museums to agriculture and beyond. One of his projects in the 1930s was an aquaculture station at Richmond Hill, where experiments were done with both bait fish and food fish. After his death in 1947, the Ford Foundation took over the station for a brief time until it was donated to the state in the early 1950s.

Today, the hatchery produces bass, bream, channel catfish, striped bass, and hybrids. Many of these fish are distributed to other states in exchange for varieties that are not as readily found in Georgia.

About 70 percent of the fish produced at the hatchery are a cross between white and striped bass. The hatchery gets its brood female stock from the nearby Ogeechee River. Workers from the hatchery go to the river and put an electrical current in the water, which stuns the fish. The fish are then netted and brought to the hatchery for spawning. Hatchery workers take egg samples and examine them under a microscope to determine when they are ready to spawn. When the eggs are ready, they are mixed with sperm in a stainless-steel jar. A mixture of salt and urea that breaks down the eggs' membrane is then added. After forty minutes, the solution is drained and replaced with tannic acid, which neutralizes the process started by the urea and salt mixture. The jars are then put on a production line and placed in water which is chilled at sixty-six degrees. It takes about forty-six hours for the eggs to hatch.

After viewing the hatchery, continue east on GA 144. You will drive through the town of Richmond Hill, which is lined with old homes and churches. It is 5.8 miles to GA 144 Spur. Turn left and head 2 miles to Hardwicke. This is a drive of spectacular beauty, with country estates and horse farms. Huge oaks hooded in moss dot both sides of the road.

In 1755, Governor John Reynolds selected this site on the Ogeechee River to be the capital of Georgia. He named it in honor of his kinsman, Philip Yorke Hardwicke, the high chancellor of England. In justifying his selection of the site, Reynolds mentioned that "Hardwicke has a charming situation, the winding of the river making it a peninsula and it is the only fit place for the capital."

But Hardwicke's fame was short-lived. The subsequent governor, James Wright, did not want the capital removed from Savannah. In 1761, he reversed the decision. This left Hardwicke as little more than a trading village. Today, it is listed among what Georgians call their state's "dead towns." Sunbury, which will be covered later in this tour, is another such dead town.

From Hardwicke, continue 1.6 miles to Fort McAllister, considered the best-preserved Confederate earthwork fortification in the country.

After the capitulation of Fort Pulaski to Union forces early in the Civil War (see The Tybee Light Tour, pages 64–67), the era of masonry fortifications came to an end. While brick structures like Fort Pulaski may look more impressive than their "earthy" counterparts, earthworks actually represent a more advanced style of fortification. Fort McAllister, begun in 1861, is a prime example of the new Confederate strategy.

The massive walls of the fort were built primarily by hand, using shovels and wheelbarrows. Though it is called a moat, the deep ditch surrounding the fort never actually held water, but rather sharpened palisades to guard against land attack. Notice the "bombproofs," or bomb shelters. These large, grass-covered mounds feature a door on the inland side, since enemy shells would come from the water. Inside were storage rooms, bedrooms, and even a fireplace. Among the fort's weapons was a "hot shot gun," which fired

Fort McAllister's earthworks

cannonballs heated to red-hot temperatures in a furnace, the objective being to set wooden ships afire.

Unfortunately, the defenders of Fort McAllister often found that their guns could not even reach the Union vessels firing at them with rifle-barreled cannons. The fort withstood a total of seven naval attacks. Perhaps the most memorable battle came on January 27, 1863, when the Union ironclad *Montauk* steamed up the Ogeechee to a position just below the fort. The *Montauk* was captained by John L. Worden, the same man who had commanded the *Monitor* in her epic clash with the *Merrimack* off North Carolina. Among the weapons at Worden's disposal was a 15-inch cannon, the largest gun ever mounted on a ship to that date. The five-hour battle on the Ogeechee was a standoff, with neither Fort McAllister nor the *Montauk* suffering much damage, a testament to the great durability of both. The following month, Worden made another attack, during which Major John B. Gallie, the commander of Fort McAllister, was killed. Amazingly, this was the fort's only fatality through the seven naval bombardments it suffered.

It finally took General William T. Sherman and his ground forces to capture Fort McAllister. The fort fell on December 13, 1864, marking the end of

Sherman's "March to the Sea." Savannah, now unprotected, was evacuated by Confederate forces shortly afterward.

Henry Ford owned Fort McAllister in the early part of this century. He began extensive restoration work on the fort in the late 1930s. Today, the fort has been restored close to the way it looked in 1865. Its museum was completed in 1963, a hundred years after some of the heaviest Union bombardment. Among its displays are shells, muskets, and other artifacts. Special reenactments are held during the year. Among the amenities at Fort McAllister and the adjoining Richmond Hill State Park are picnic areas, shelters, restrooms, and facilities for tent and trailer camping.

Fort McAllister is also known for its Fourth of July barbecue, which is attended by thousands of tourists and local citizens. It seems as if every region of the South has its own brand of barbecue, and Georgia is no exception. Over seven thousand people attend the festivities, consuming over sixty-eight hundred pounds of barbecue.

Georgia barbecue aficionados suggest that a barbecue pit should be 1½ feet deep, 4 feet wide, and 5 feet long. The fire in the pit should be of green oak wood, from a tree that is not too large. The wood must be burned to red coals before the pit is ready for the pig. The pig's head is removed near the shoulders, and the feet are removed just above the first joint. Iron rods are run lengthwise through the hams and shoulders so that both ends of the rods rest on the banks of the pit. The rods are inserted near the skin and under the ribs in order to lower the neck, shoulders, and hams into the pit. The pig must be watched carefully and basted frequently. Although most cooks carefully guard their variations on the basting sauce, the basic Georgia recipe contains apple vinegar, dry mustard, Worcestershire sauce, catsup, chili sauce, lemon juice, brown sugar, and butter.

To continue the tour, retrace your route to I-95 and turn south. After 13.3 miles, take Exit 13. The main tour heads west on U.S. 84/GA 38 from Exit 13. Martin's Glebe Plantation is on the right.

It is 1.6 miles from Exit 13 to Midway (sometimes spelled Medway). Turn north onto U.S. 17 and continue 0.4 mile to Midway Congregational Church. The church is on the right, the cemetery on the left, and a museum just beyond the church. Residents of Midway and surrounding Liberty County—St. John's Parish in the days before Georgia was organized into counties—are a mite smug about this church. They have every right to be.

Midway Congregational Church was founded by a group of Puritans who were descendants of the English colony that arrived in Massachusetts in 1630.

Some of these Puritans migrated to South Carolina and later became interested in Georgia as its economy expanded.

Three scouts were sent to look for locations in Georgia in May 1752. They were followed by five more in June. The scouts were so pleased with the location they called Midway that they went to Savannah and obtained land grants totaling nearly 32,000 acres. The first settlers—Benjamin Baker, Samuel Bacon, and their families—arrived later that year to begin a settlement.

Soon, a community of three hundred sprang up, and the surrounding plantations were growing rice by the ton. In 1754, the people of Midway erected a church. When trouble began to brew between the American colonies and England, the citizens around Midway and St. John's Parish were outspoken in their support for American rights. Many local residents were leaders in the independence movement. The story is told that the original church in Midway was used as a meeting place for some of the local Revolutionary leaders.

As the war progressed, the British invaded Georgia from Florida. In 1778, they burned the church. The present structure dates from 1792.

Matilda Harden Stevens was one of the last living persons who had attended Midway Church before the Civil War. Her reminiscences, written shortly before the turn of the century, were published in the *Georgia Historical Quarterly* in 1944. Mrs. Stevens described the drive from her home to the church this way:

> Our drive was over broad, level roads, beautifully kept and bordered by magnificent forests which alternated with fields of cotton, still white long after the frost had changed the green of their leaves and stalks to brown. Here and there we rolled over long causeways and sounding bridges as we crossed the swamps that stretched their arms far into the region of pineland. . . . From the dark swamp, through a long arch of overhanging boughs, we caught the first glimpse of Midway Church. There it was, its white wall shining in the sunlight, its steeple towering aloft.

Here is her description of the interior of the church during a service: "The pews were divided into four groups, two of which are arranged longitudinally, while the other two were at right angles to these, but facing the pulpit and separated by it.

"In the early times, the pews of our church were large and high,—so high, indeed, that only the heads of the grown people were visible. To us little ones, they were veritable boxes, allowing us to see only the minister and thereby inculcating a truly devotional spirit."

During the Civil War, Union troops came through Midway, confiscated all the livestock, burned all the crops, and used the church as a slaughterhouse. With no food, most of the residents drifted away from the area and never returned. The last official meeting at Midway Church was held in December 1865.

Today, the church is used occasionally for weddings and funerals and special events like Easter sunrise services and homecomings for the descendants of the original settlers. It is open to the public every day. The church has recently undergone extensive renovation sponsored by the Midway Society, a non-profit organization largely composed of descendants of the settlers. The efforts to maintain the old structure have even included wrapping bands around the church to keep its inevitable cracks from spreading.

It is still a source of pride that during the 111 years the original and current versions of Midway Church were in active use, the congregation counted among its members two signers of the Declaration of Independence, one United States minister to a foreign country, six congressmen, four governors, eighty-two ministers—including the fathers of Oliver Wendell Holmes and Samuel Morse—six foreign missionaries, two university chancellors, six professors, four authors, and miscellaneous scientists, inventors, teachers, attorneys, and doctors. In the opinion of many, the people of Midway Church, the surrounding community, and St. John's Parish were the moral and intellectual nobility of Georgia.

The church cemetery, located across the road from the church, bears out this view. It is the final resting place of several important people in Georgia history.

One of these was General Daniel Stewart, who joined the patriot army at age fifteen, later distinguished himself in the Indian wars, and served in the Georgia legislature for several years. But his greatest claim to fame may be that he was the great-grandfather of Theodore Roosevelt. Fort Stewart, a nearby army base, was named in his honor.

Another Revolutionary War hero buried here is General James Screven, the captain of the St. John's Rangers and later brigadier general of the Georgia forces. He was killed in a skirmish with the British about a mile south of the church in 1778. The tall monument in the middle of the cemetery is dedicated to Screven and Stewart.

Matilda Harden Stevens described some lesser-known figures who found their final resting place in this cemetery:

Midway Congregational Church

One enclosure contained the graves of the four successive wives of one man lying peacefully side by side. I used to wonder if I could have slept peacefully under like circumstances. One inscription, and only one, do I remember: "He was not, for God took him." It was one of whom I never knew. He was said to have been a good man who was killed by lightning. This made a great impression on me. God took him, like Enoch of old, without the pain, the languishing of disease, the dread of crossing the narrow stream into that unknown land, the anguish of parting with loved ones; one moment here, the next with God. Truly a fitting inscription!

Mrs. Stevens told of another grave containing the remains of a man who committed suicide. It seems the victim was in love with two women. When he could not decide which of the two to marry, he ended his "perplexity," as Mrs. Stevens called it, by "committing the awful deed." Since a suicide victim could not be buried on hallowed ground, the man was buried outside the wall. Over the years, the wall enclosing the burial ground was enlarged until his grave was finally inside the cemetery.

The cemetery was laid out soon after the original church was erected in 1754.

Midway Congregational Church cemetery

The brick wall encircling it was built in 1813. The wall is six feet high and eighteen inches thick. The bricks used in the wall were shipped from England and completely plastered over. Historians believe the cemetery contains about twelve hundred graves, but it is hard to determine the exact number because so many of the cypress markers have deteriorated with time.

There is an interesting story about the cemetery wall that explains the crack in the north side of Section A. Supposedly, the wall was built by slave labor, with each planter furnishing his slaves for a few days. One day, two slaves began quarreling and failed to finish their tasks. The overseer sent the others home but left these two to finish their work. The quarrel escalated until one finally killed the other. The surviving slave buried his victim and laid bricks over his body. He then reported that his adversary had run away. Within days, the wall cracked. It was repaired but cracked again. Years later, when the body was discovered, people assumed the wall could be mended without cracking. However, it continued to crack each time it was repaired.

Next to the church is the Midway Museum, which houses exhibits, documents, and furnishings from the colonial period through the last official meeting at the church late in the Civil War.

After viewing Midway Congregational Church and its cemetery and museum, retrace your route to I-95. Cross the interstate and continue 2.2 miles on U.S. 84/GA 38 to the historical marker on the right for Dorchester. Turn right and drive 0.2 mile to Dorchester Presbyterian Church, on the left.

The village of Dorchester was settled in 1843 by families from Midway and Sunbury. Although the village no longer survives, Dorchester Presbyterian Church is still very much in existence. Built in 1854, it was initially used only for summer services. In 1871, it was admitted to the Savannah presbytery with a membership of fourteen. The bell was originally used in Sunbury. The font and communion service were moved here after Midway Church ceased hosting services.

After viewing Dorchester Presbyterian Church, return to U.S. 84/GA 38 and continue 2.2 miles to a sign for Fort Morris Historical Site. If you wish to make a brief side trip to visit the area's newest attraction, head east on U.S. 84/GA38. Follow the signs for Seabrook School, a living farm museum that preserves the traditions and crafts of rural African-Americans around the turn of the century. This ambitious project began in 1991 with the restoration of the historic one-room Seabrook School. The tour continues by turning at the sign for Fort Morris and proceeding 2.5 miles to Fort Morris, located on the right.

Midway Museum

TOURING THE COASTAL GEORGIA BACKROADS

You are also on the site of what was once Sunbury; this is another of Georgia's "dead towns." Not one vestige is left of the colonial town that rose on the slopes of the river. The streets, squares, and marketplace of the town have completely vanished. Today, weeds choke the deserted docks where vessels used to land rich cargo.

As the plantations of Midway and St. John's Parish prospered, there was a real need for a local shipping port. Overland transportation to Savannah was precarious and expensive. In the mid-1750s, some industrious citizens led by Captain Mark Carr undertook to build their own port on the banks of the Midway River. (For more information on Mark Carr, see The Marshes of Glynn Tour, page 127.)

Dorchester Presbyterian Church

From the start, the new town of Sunbury was a thriving place. Naturalist William Bartram visited in the mid-1760s on his well-documented travels through the Southeast and described the town as having "pleasant piazzas around [its houses] where the genteel, wealthy planters resorted to partake of the sea breeze, bathing and sporting on the Sea Islands."

By that time, the community boasted 80 homes, a custom house, a naval office, and several businesses. Prior to the Revolution, Sunbury was second only to Savannah in the number of waterborne exports leaving Georgia. In 1773, the port cleared 56 vessels, while Savannah cleared 160.

Like the rest of St. John's Parish, Sunbury was caught up in the revolutionary fever of the early 1770s. When the Declaration of Independence was signed, all three signers from Georgia—Dr. Lyman Hall, Button Gwinnett, and George Walton—were from St. John's Parish.

But Sunbury paid a high price for its loyalty to the American cause.

At the beginning of the hostilities, Fort Morris was erected to guard the town and St. John's Parish. The fort was an enclosed earthwork shaped like an irregular quadrangle. Surrounded by a parapet and a moat, it contained a parade area of about an acre. More than twenty-five pieces of ordnance of varying size defended the fort, which was garrisoned early in 1776. During the war, the Americans launched three invasions of British-held east Florida from Fort Morris.

On November 25, 1778, some 500 British ground troops supported by armed ships in the Midway River landed at Sunbury and demanded the immediate surrender of Fort Morris. Although there were only 127 troops and a total of fewer than 200 men inside the fort, counting local citizens, the commander of the garrison, Colonel John McIntosh, challenged the British with a defiant reply: "Come and take it!" The British retreated on that occasion. Years later, as an expression of gratitude, the Georgia legislature presented McIntosh with a sword inscribed with his famous words.

The British returned six weeks later. This time, they would not be bluffed. Major Joseph Lane, the new commander of Fort Morris, was ordered to evacuate, but urged by the citizens of Sunbury to stay and defend the fort, he disobeyed his superiors. The Americans suffered four dead and seven wounded in the ensuing battle against superior British forces. Fort Morris was surrendered on January 8, 1779. Major Lane was later court-martialed for his disobedience.

With the fall of this last coastal defense, the British swept through Georgia, capturing several of the colony's finest military leaders. The British then converted Sunbury into something of a military prison. Patriot leaders were paroled on their honor and allowed to circulate freely within the limits of the town. George Walton, acting commander of the Georgia militia at that time, was one of these prisoners.

Although the area remained under British control until April 1782, the redcoats and their prisoners withdrew from Sunbury in October 1779.

The port never recovered its prewar prosperity. For a time, Sunbury served as a summer getaway, but that was simply another step on the road to decline. Most of the residents had fled. The British had burned or otherwise destroyed the fort and most of the town. And Georgia's economy began to change in the early 1800s. People and commerce began to move inland. Rice, ideally suited for the swampy area around Sunbury, was replaced by cotton as the major crop. New railroads were built, but they passed well inland of town. By the mid-1800s, Sunbury was pretty well deserted. Nonetheless, the town is still remembered as the homeplace of the Georgia signers of the Declaration of Independence.

Fort Morris earthworks

For over a hundred years, Fort Morris lay lonely and forgotten beneath the moss-festooned oaks. The Georgia Historical Commission acquired it in 1968. The fort was placed on the National Register of Historic Places in 1971. Today, a museum in the visitor center displays memorabilia of the American Revolution.

From the grounds of Fort Morris Historic Site, you can see St. Catherines and Ossabaw islands. Although neither is open to the public, their histories are worth relating.

St. Catherines Island and St. Simons Island, farther to the south, are probably the most historic of coastal Georgia's Golden Isles. St. Catherines, visible on the right from Fort Morris, has a history that predates the earliest European exploration of North and South America. The capital of the Creek Indian confederacy was located on the island. There were also several other Native American settlements on the 25,000-acre landmass.

In recognition of the island's importance to the local Indians, Spanish authorities established the Santa Catalina de Guale mission on St. Catherines in 1566. First run by the Jesuits and later by the Franciscans, the mission was finally abandoned in the mid-1600s after several bloody Indian uprisings.

After James Oglethorpe landed at what was to become Savannah in 1733, his relations with local Native Americans were greatly aided by Mary Musgrove, also known as Coosaponakesee, a half-Creek, half-white woman who operated a trading post in the area. Musgrove acted as an interpreter between the white settlers and the local Indians. For her services in bringing about a treaty that allowed white settlers to peacefully coexist with the Indians, she was granted ownership of Ossabaw, St. Catherines, and Sapelo islands. Since she was a niece of one of the Creek chiefs, the treaty refers to her as a "princess." She later married Thomas Bosomworth, a preacher from England who was sent to minister to the new colonists.

When Georgia finally agreed to allow slavery in 1749, the islands granted to Mary Musgrove became desirable as plantation lands. The colony's trustees disputed the Bosomworths' ownership claim, which led to a decade-long legal struggle.

At one point during the dispute, the Bosomworths and their Indian allies made a show of force. In *Georgia's Land of the Golden Isles*, Burnette Vanstory describes what must have been an unusual scene: "Led by the princess in her royal trappings and Thomas Bosomworth in his canonical robes, two hundred Indian braves marched into the seaport city [Savannah], where they remained for a fortnight threatening the authorities and intimidating residents."

Even though the case was still in the courts, Thomas and Mary Bosomworth cleared and planted fields on St. Catherines and began the construction of a fine home. In 1760, the couple was officially granted ownership of St. Catherines Island, while the other islands in dispute were purchased by England. Mary lived only a few more years.

In the 1760s, Thomas Bosomworth sold the island to Button Gwinnett, one of colonial Georgia's most colorful figures.

Gwinnett learned of the port of Savannah, Georgia, while living in England.

In 1765, he sailed to Savannah and bought an export firm there. His wife joined him in 1767. They settled on St. Catherines and began to develop an extensive plantation. The couple had three daughters, but only one, Elizabeth, survived to maturity.

Gwinnett had bought St. Catherines entirely on credit. By 1773, he was so badly in debt that his creditors forced him to sell the island to pay his debts. At that point, he moved his family to Savannah.

By 1774, anti-British sentiment was growing in the colony. Most thought Gwinnett was loyal to the crown because of his English ties. However, when an open meeting was held at Tondee's Tavern in Savannah in July 1774, Gwinnett was present.

On February 2, 1776, Gwinnett, Dr. Lyman Hall, and George Walton were chosen as Georgia's delegates to the Continental Congress. With Walton arranging to travel later, Gwinnett and Hall made the 800-mile journey to Philadelphia together, arriving on May 20. On that day, John Adams noted that "the delegates from Georgia made their appearance this day in Congress with unlimited powers, and these gentlemen are very firm." Years later, in his autobiography, Adams characterized the two Georgians as intelligent, spirited men "who made a powerful addition to our Phalanx."

As revolutionary sentiments escalated, friendships sometimes became strained. Gwinnett and General Lachlan McIntosh, a native of Scotland and a prominent military figure in Georgia, had long been good friends. But in January 1777, Gwinnett, back in Savannah, received a confidential communication from John Hancock, the president of the Continental Congress. Hancock informed Gwinnett that George McIntosh, the general's brother, was conniving with the British.

Gwinnett immediately arranged for George McIntosh's arrest. Later, the Georgia Safety Council reviewed the matter and released McIntosh. But his brother, the general, was furious. He called Gwinnett "a scoundrel and a rascal."

According to the custom of the time, Gwinnett sent Lachlan McIntosh a challenge, requesting that McIntosh meet him early on the morning of May 16, 1777. McIntosh replied that the hour was earlier than he usually arose, but that he would gladly meet the challenger at the appointed time.

They met less than 0.5 mile from the center of Savannah. When a crowd gathered, the dueling site was moved downhill to a safer location. The weapons were checked to determine that each had a single bullet. The men agreed to fire from a distance of four paces. When one of the seconds proposed that the antagonists stand back to back, McIntosh objected, saying, "By no means. Let us see what we are about."

They faced each other. At the agreed-upon signal, they fired simultaneously. Gwinnett was shot above the knee, his bone badly fractured. McIntosh was shot through the leg muscle but not seriously wounded. He called to Gwinnett, asking if he wished to stand for another shot. "Yes, if they will help me up," Gwinnett answered. The seconds objected. McIntosh was finally assisted to where Gwinnett lay, and the two gentlemen shook hands. They were then removed to their homes.

Gwinnett developed gangrene in his wounded leg and died on the morning of May 19, 1777, three days after the duel. Dr. Lyman Hall, fellow signer of the Declaration of Independence, was among those who mourned. "O Liberty," he wrote. "Why do you suffer so many of your faithful sons, your warmest votaries, to fall at your shrine. Alas, my friend, my friend!" Charles C. Jones, Jr., the author of a biographical sketch of Gwinnett, characterized him this way: "Brief but brilliant was the career of Button Gwinnett. Rising like a meteor, he shot athwart the zenith of the young commonwealth, concentrating the gaze of all, and, in a short moment, was seen no more."

Public sentiment against Lachlan McIntosh ran so high that he was run out of Georgia for two years, though he later distinguished himself in George Washington's army.

Because there are only thirty-six known examples of his signature, one of which is on the Declaration of Independence, Gwinnett's autograph brings extraordinarily high prices at auction. In 1924, a letter bearing his name was purchased for $14,000. In 1943, one of his signatures held in a vault in the state treasury was appraised at $52,000.

For someone whose signature appears on our country's most famous document, Button Gwinnett remains a man of many mysteries. The date of his birth is unknown. Some believe he grew up in Wales, while others say he grew up farther east in Gloucester, near Birmingham, England. His signature on the Declaration became a subject of controversy many years after the fact, when it was postulated that "Button" was actually "Bulton" and that "Gwinnett" was a pseudonym. No one knows what he looked like. There is no written description or authentic portrait of Button Gwinnett, not even in John Trumbull's famous group painting of the signers of the Declaration. Even his burial site has been disputed.

After Gwinnett's death, Thomas Bosomworth returned to St. Catherines with his second wife. He lived there for the rest of his life. In 1800, St.

Catherines became the property of Jacob Walburg, an industrious man who developed two plantations on the island.

The island was abandoned during the Civil War. Immediately following the war, General Sherman created an independent state encompassing all the sea islands between Charleston and the St. Johns River in Florida. Created for the freed slaves from those islands, this separatist state was governed by a man named Tunis Campbell and had its capital at St. Catherines. Congress repealed Sherman's directive a few years later, and the short-lived state ceased to exist.

The island then passed through a succession of owners, including Howard Coffin, the owner of nearby Sapelo Island, who purchased St. Catherines in 1927. It was Coffin who carefully restored and enlarged the so-called Old House, which tradition claims was the home of Button Gwinnett. In 1943, the island was purchased by Edward J. Noble. Following his death, it came under the ownership of the Edward J. Noble Foundation.

Since 1974, the New York Zoological Society has used St. Catherines as a sanctuary for rare and endangered species. Exotic animals such as gray zebras, sable antelopes, and hartebeests wander the fields.

Today, St. Catherines is also the site of a major archaeological dig that is slowly uncovering the ruins of Santa Catalina de Guale, the sixteenth-century Spanish mission. St. Catherines was once the capital of the Guale Indian nation. The American Museum of Natural History is one of the sponsors of this effort.

Ossabaw Island, the other island visible from Fort Morris, is the northernmost of Georgia's Golden Isles. It was also the site of the first great plantation empire on the Georgia coast.

After early ownership by Mary Musgrove and Thomas Bosomworth, the entire island was purchased by John Morel in 1760. Morel was an experienced planter who had settled along the Ashley River in South Carolina in 1730. Morel's slaves cleared the fields of Ossabaw Island and planted vast quantities of indigo, which was used as a dye. Morel soon acquired a nice fortune from his indigo plantation. One interesting custom of the slaves at the indigo plantations along coastal South Carolina and Georgia involved the indigo paint that can still be seen on some houses in the area. The slaves, probably drawing from their African traditions, believed that evil spirits could not go through anything painted blue. The laborers often used the skimmings off the indigo vats to paint the doors and shutters of their churches and homes.

During the Revolution, the Morel family became ardent supporters of the

American cause. Often, endangered patriots fled to the island, knowing they would find sanctuary there.

After the war, timbering became a prime industry on Ossabaw Island. Late in his life, John Morel divided his island into three plantations, which were eventually inherited by his three sons.

In the early 1800s, sea-island cotton was introduced to Ossabaw Island. Burnette Vanstory thus describes life on the island in those years: "Ossabaw fields were white with cotton, her wharves busy with barges, schooners and boats of happy groups for house parties and hunting parties. . . . In those days when the coastal planters had 'company for breakfast, dinner, tea and supper, and drawing rooms were lighted by whole dozens of spermaceti candles high blazing from glass chandeliers,' a beautiful custom in the Morel family was the molding of the candles of Ossabaw."

By the early 1850s, most of the island had passed out of the Morel family's ownership. During the Civil War, a Union battery was located on Ossabaw's northern tip for a short while, but the island was mostly deserted.

During the early 1900s, the island was purchased and used as a hunting preserve by the Wanamaker family of Philadelphia. In 1924, it was sold to Dr. H. N. Torrey of Michigan. Torrey rounded up the wild cattle and hogs that were running free and built a grand Spanish-style home on the north end; this home still stands. The first person to sign the guest book was Henry Ford.

In 1961, Eleanor Torrey West formed the Ossabaw Foundation, which undertook the ambitious Ossabaw Island Project. This project sponsored several artistic and environmental-research communities on the island. In 1978, the island was sold to the state, which took over the management of the foundation's programs. At one time, students from more than twenty colleges and universities were participating in the foundation's various programs. During the 1980s, much of the important ecological work of the project was abandoned due to lack of funds.

Today, the island is managed by the Georgia Department of Natural Resources as the Ossabaw Island Heritage Preserve. The land is used only for natural, scientific, and cultural purposes based on environmentally sound practices.

This tour ends with the view of St. Catherines and Ossabaw islands from the grounds of Fort Morris.

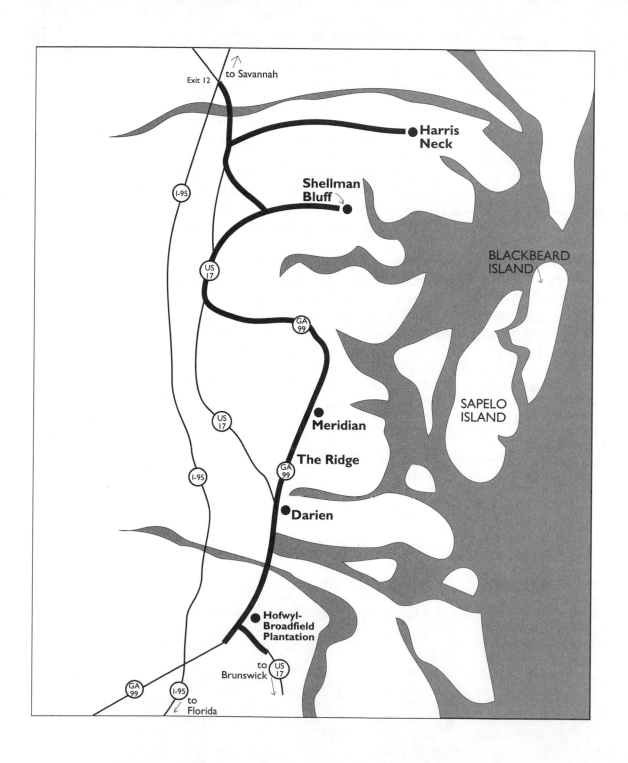

The Planters Tour

This tour begins at Hofwyl-Broadfield Plantation and continues to Youth Estate, Butler Island, Darien, Fort King George, The Ridge, and Meridian. It then goes by boat to Sapelo Island and returns to Meridien. It proceeds to Shellman Bluff before ending at the chapel known as "The Smallest Church in Georgia."

Total mileage: approximately 51 miles.

The tour begins at Hofwyl-Broadfield Plantation State Historic Site, located on U.S. 17 approximately 15 miles north of Brunswick.

In 1803, William Brailsford, an Englishman, bought Broughton, a rice island on the south branch of the Altamaha River. He and his wife, Maria Heyward, whose family owned more South Carolina plantations than anyone else at that time, settled on the island the following year. Shortly after they arrived, a powerful hurricane crashed ashore, destroying their house and killing approximately seventy slaves, who, due to the negligence of their overseer, were not moved to shelter in time. Major Pierce Butler from neighboring Butler Island offered the use of his house until the Brailsfords were able to rebuild. From that day, there were close ties between the two plantations. When construction of the Brailsfords' house was completed, the family returned to its plantation.

Over the years, the Brailsford offspring married into some of Georgia's most prominent families. William and Maria's daughter Camilla married the brother of Governor George Troup. The daughter of this union was Ophelia Troup, who married George Dent, the son of a retired naval commander. Ten years after their marriage at Broadfield Plantation, Ophelia and George Dent came to Broadfield to live. In 1851, George built a new house which he named Hofwyl, after the school he had attended in Switzerland. This two-story frame house with shuttered windows still stands on the property.

After the Civil War, Hofwyl-Broadfield, as it was commonly called, was almost in ruins. When George Dent did not feel up to the task, Ophelia's sister Matilda offered to rebuild the house.

The next family member to inherit the plantation was James Dent, the eldest son of George and Ophelia. In 1880, James married Miriam Cohen, who proved to be such an astute businesswoman that all business matters were transacted in her name.

During his tenure, James observed that it was probably mosquitoes—not "bad air" rising from the low-lying rice fields, as was commonly believed—that caused malaria, which claimed many lives during the humid summer months. He announced that his family would not join the other coastal planters who fled to higher altitudes during the summer. He had black iron screens installed on all the windows and doors and remained on his plantation during the summer. When other families returned in the fall, they immediately asked who had died. But the Dent family had survived the dreaded fever season intact.

After James's death, Miriam became a woman rice planter. In 1917, the rice plantation was converted to a dairy farm. After their mother's death, Miriam's two daughters, Ophelia and Miriam, took over the duties of the dairy operation. Miriam capped the milk bottles and made butter, while Ophelia took responsibility for making deliveries. The sisters finally closed the operation in 1942, having attained financial security. "Miss Ophelia" lived on the property until her death in 1973 at age eighty-six. She left the 1,268-acre plantation to the state of Georgia.

In June 1979, it was opened as a state historic site. Please note that the site is closed on Mondays.

House at
Hofwyl-Broadfield Plantation

TOURING THE COASTAL GEORGIA BACKROADS

Visitors can begin their tour of the property at the museum adjacent to the parking lot. There, they can view a model of a working rice plantation. Silver is also on display. The exhibits and slide show tell about the lives of the rice planters and their slaves.

From the museum, you can walk or ride to the mansion and its outbuildings. If you walk, you will follow the brick walkway that once led from the dairy barn and milk house to the back door of the plantation house. When it rained, the pasture near the house became quite muddy from the heavy traffic of the grazing cows. This narrow walkway helped to clean off some of that mud when workers traveled from the house to the outbuildings.

Among the several outbuildings open for touring is the bottling house, where fresh, warm milk from the adjacent dairy barn was brought twice a day in five-gallon milk cans. The milk was weighed to record the daily output of each cow. Then it was put in bottles and capped by a bottling machine. Originally, the bottled milk was stored in a large cooler with an ice locker on top. It was later replaced by a refrigerator powered by a combination of gas and electricity.

The dairy barn once housed thirty-five Jersey and Guernsey cows that produced 100 to 150 bottles of milk daily. The milk was delivered to residences all over the area—including a daily delivery of forty to fifty gallons to millionaires vacationing on nearby Jekyll Island during the winter months.

The pay shed was built after the Civil War. It was there that black laborers received payment for their services, reflecting the change in their status after the abolition of slavery.

On the way to the house, you will pass a brick wall with a fancy wrought-iron gate. This gate was designed to keep curious cows out of what was once the laundry yard.

When you reach the house, ring the front doorbell for a guided tour of the premises. The house is decorated just as it was when "Miss Ophelia" lived here. In fact, the bedspreads she crocheted are still on the beds.

After touring the historic site, return to U.S. 17 and turn right. Turn left almost immediately onto GA 99. Travel 0.4 mile to Youth Estate, also known as Elizafield Plantation.

Located along the Altamaha River, Elizafield Plantation was the home of Dr. Robert Grant, a native of Scotland who lived in South Carolina for several years before coming to Georgia. In the 1790s, Grant purchased Elizafield, Grantley, and Evelyn plantations, all properties that had been confiscated during the Revolutionary War. Elizafield later passed to his son, Hugh Fraser

Grant, one of the wealthiest planters of the early nineteenth century. Elizafield was planted primarily in rice and sugar cane.   The plantation was the subject of considerable confusion in the first half of the twentieth century. For a time, the ruins of the Grant family's sugar plant were mistakenly thought to be the remains of a Spanish mission dating from around 1604. In the 1930s, 350 acres of the property were even donated to the state to be designated as Santo Domingo State Park.

When the historical inaccuracy was revealed and the state-park project fell through, the Georgia legislature made the property available for the establishment of a Boys' Town similar to the famous Nebraska institution. The boys who lived here elected their own "city" officials and even had their own chamber of commerce. One of the most popular parts of the town was called "Dogs' Estate"; each boy was allowed to have a dog, and Dogs' Estate was where those dogs stayed. When girls were admitted in 1976, the name of the complex was changed to Youth Estate.

Today, the property is privately run. The old Spanish-style stucco buildings, with their arches and red tile roofs, make interesting viewing.

After exploring Youth Estate, return to U.S. 17 and turn north. Drive 3.6 miles to see the rice plantation on Butler Island.

This island is named for Pierce Butler, who came to America in 1765 as a major in the Twenty-ninth British Regiment. In 1771, Butler married Mary "Polly" Middleton, a member of one of South Carolina's most prestigious families. Butler then retired from the army and took up life as a plantation master.

When the American Revolution began, he joined the colonial cause. After the war, he served as a South Carolina delegate to the Constitutional Convention. He was one of that state's signers of the Constitution, as well as one of its first United States senators, an office he held for several terms.

During his tenure as senator, Butler lived in Philadelphia, but he owned three large tracts in coastal Georgia. Woodville, on the mainland, was not cultivated. Hampton Plantation, also known as Butler Point, became a sea-island cotton plantation (see The Marshes of Glynn Tour, pages 139–41). The third tract was Butler Island, a rice plantation located at the delta of the Altamaha River.

In his later years, Butler's greatest wish was that the family name be carried on. After his death in 1822, his will directed that his Georgia property pass to any of his grandsons—the children of his daughter, Sarah Butler, and her husband, Dr. James Mease—with the stipulation that whichever of the boys wanted to be his heir had to change his last name. One grandson died in boyhood. Another, John, favored retaining the name Mease. But fifteen-year-old Butler Mease legally took the name Pierce Butler II and inherited the property. Years later, John decided to change his name as well, and Pierce conveyed him half the Georgia property.

Although this second Pierce Butler became a prosperous planter, his reputation came largely from being the man who married Fanny Kemble.

Frances Anne Kemble, better known as "Fanny," was a noted English actress when she arrived in the United States in 1832 to tour the country with her father. Immensely popular, she was accepted into the high society of all the cities she visited.

But it was Pierce Butler who won her heart. After their marriage in 1834, Fanny retired from the stage.

In 1838, Pierce planned a business trip to see his plantations. Fanny was interested in seeing the land and the slaves who worked the large tracts. They and their two children—Sarah, age three, and Frances, age six months—left for Georgia.

The family stayed at Butler Island for nearly two months. Fanny had asked a friend, Elizabeth Dwight Sedgwick, to join them in Georgia. When Elizabeth was unable to come, Fanny promised to keep a journal of what she witnessed. And Fanny did not like much of what she saw.

Butler Island was highly suitable for the production of rice. Near the coast, freshwater rivers such as the Altamaha are affected by the rise and fall of tides twice during every twenty-four-hour period, providing a natural irrigation system for the fields. But the land is far enough inland that the river is not invaded by salt water, which would destroy the crop and ruin the fields for years to come.

The rice industry along the Altamaha River reached its peak between 1800 and 1860. By the end of 1838, when Pierce Butler and his family came visiting, there were some 280,000 slaves in Georgia, or more than 50 percent of the state's population. Indeed, Georgia had one of the densest concentrations of slaves in the entire country. In McIntosh County, where Butler Island is located, slaves comprised over 80 percent of the population.

Fanny and Pierce had stormy quarrels concerning the institution of slavery. Fanny also made her dislike for slavery crystal-clear in her journal. When they returned to Philadelphia, Fanny and Pierce separated, and Fanny returned to the stage. They finally divorced in 1840, and Pierce was granted custody of their children.

In the 1850s, Pierce faced financial ruin. He was accused of irresponsible management of his Georgia plantations and was forced to sell nearly half his slaves at auction.

By the time the Civil War broke out, Fanny was hearing expressions of sympathy for the Confederacy and defenses of the institution of slavery. She became determined to publish her journal to show slavery in its true light. Her *Journal of a Residence on a Georgian Plantation, 1838–39* was published in England in May 1863. A few months later, it was published by Harper Brothers in this country. Promotional hyperbole called the book "the most thrilling and remarkable picture of the interior social life of the slaveholding section of this country that has ever been published." Needless to say, it created a stir. A classic work, it remains in print today.

After the war, Pierce Butler and his daughter Frances returned to Butler Island to try to revive the plantation. The old overseer's cottage where Fanny Kemble Butler had written her journal was still there. Frances Butler brought the furniture out of storage and made the rooms cozy. In 1866, the plantation had its best rice crop ever, but Pierce Butler died before the harvest was in.

Frances stayed on to manage the property for several years. Following in her mother's footsteps, she wrote *Ten Years on a Georgia Plantation*, an interesting and valuable account of life on the Georgia coast during Reconstruction. While she lived on the island, she was often visited by her sister Sarah's son, Owen Wister, who later carried on the family tradition of authorship when he

Butler Island Rice Plantation with brick chimney from rice mill in the foreground

penned the novel *The Virginian.*

In 1926, Butler Island and its neighbor, Champney Island, were purchased by Colonel T. L. Huston, who was half-owner of the New York Yankees when Babe Ruth was a national celebrity. Huston installed a new system of dikes and canals designed by engineers from Holland. He then planted the fields in iceberg lettuce, beans, cauliflower, and cabbage. He also collected a herd of Guernsey and Holstein cows and started a dairy. By 1953, twenty-five thousand crates of "Great Lakes" iceberg lettuce were being shipped from Butler Island annually. No farming is done on the property today.

Huston also constructed the two-story Colonial-style mansion on the island. He and his wife became popular residents of the area. Mrs. Huston was a regular bridge partner of Miss Ophelia Troup Dent of nearby Hofwyl Plantation.

As you approach the rice plantation on Butler Island today, you will see a high chimney on the left. This 75-foot brick chimney is the remnant of a steam-powered rice mill that was built by slaves in the 1850s. As you continue on the loop around the plantation, you will notice a second chimney. This one was part of a tide-powered rice mill. The white house in the background is not the original plantation manor built by Pierce Butler, but Colonel Huston's house, built in 1926. Visitors may also view the system of dikes and canals that supplied the rice fields with water in days gone by.

Butler Island is now part of the 21,000-acre Altamaha Wildlife Management Area. Located on the Atlantic Flyway, the area is best known for its bird population. More than seventeen species of ducks inhabit the area depending upon the season, along with wading birds, furbearers, and a variety of other wildlife.

After driving the loop around the plantation, continue north on U.S. 17. You will soon cross a bridge over the Butler River. It is 1 mile from the plantation to the Darien River Bridge, which leads into the town of Darien. After the bridge, you will see the McIntosh County Chamber of Commerce and the Darien Welcome Center on the right. This is the place to pick up a map for a tour of Darien. Also make sure you purchase tickets for the ferry to Sapelo Island if you want to make that trip; this is the only outlet for ferry tickets.

Although the trip to Sapelo Island is highly recommended, it is not something that can be done on impulse. You can only visit the island as part of a guided tour, as the guest of a resident, or as an attendee at a conference. If you wish to take the guided tour, you must check to make sure tours are offered on the day you wish to go. Although tours run more frequently in the summer than at other times, they are not offered every day. There is usually only one tour on tour days, and it leaves the dock in Meridien at 8:30 A.M. You can arrange an all-day tour or a half-day tour at the welcome center in Darien. If you wish to make advance reservations—a good idea, since the tour is popular—call 912-473-6684 or 912-437-4192.

Settlement in the Darien area began in 1721 with the building of Fort King George. John "Tuscarora Jack" Barnwell of Beaufort, South Carolina, believed that a fort was necessary between Port Royal, South Carolina, and St. Augustine, Florida, to counteract French and Spanish expansion. Barnwell and his Carolina Rangers built a cypress blockhouse twenty-six feet square and twenty-three feet high. The fort included palisaded earthworks, a moat, and thatched huts for barracks.

Replica of blockhouse at Fort King George

For seven years, British soldiers garrisoned the fort, enduring incredible hardships from disease, insects, and weather. The soldiers had little or no fresh fruit and vegetables in their diet. Meat preserved by salting rotted in the humid weather. By the end of the first year, two-thirds of the company had perished. During an excavation of the fort begun in 1940, unmarked graves were discovered. Today, each contains a marker bearing the inscription "Soldier of Fort King George."

By 1735, James Oglethorpe realized he needed more of a presence in this area to stave off Spanish expansion. A group of Highland Scots was recruited from the vicinity of Inverness, Scotland, to settle the land at the mouth of the Altamaha River. When the Scots arrived in January 1736, they cruised up the

Altamaha to Fort King George, then followed a tidal creek east to Sapelo Sound. There, they built homes for themselves and set out to defend the southern English frontier in America against all enemies. Records show there were 177 men in this original party. Tomo-chi-chi sent six Indians as guides and hunters. (For more information about Tomo-chi-chi, see The Lincoln's Christmas Gift Tour, pages 23–25.)

When Oglethorpe arrived back in Georgia after a trip to England, he came to this area to select a site for a fort. Upon his arrival, the Scottish troops paraded in full costume, with bonnets, plaids, targets, broadswords, and firearms. It is believed that the Highlanders became Oglethorpe's favorite colonists.

The new fort—Fort Darien—was 60 miles from Savannah and 90 miles from Spanish fortifications. Supposedly, it was so strong that forty men could hold it against three hundred.

In choosing a name for the new settlement, the Scots honored an earlier Scottish settlement located on what was then called the Isthmus of Darien—now the Isthmus of Panama. Scottish colonists sailed there in 1698. Records from early Spanish explorers show that the four-month voyage, conflicts with Spanish raiding parties, and fever-laden quagmires and jungles took their toll on the new settlement. By 1699, the colony was abandoned. Of the 1,200 men who sailed from Scotland, 744 were dead, and the rest were incapacitated by sickness. The Scots in Georgia welcomed the opportunity to take on the Spanish again, perhaps even to extract some vengeance for their failure in what is now Panama.

If the Scots came to Darien looking for a fight, they found it. The year 1739 saw the beginning of a protracted conflict with the Spanish. Early in that conflict, ninety-five Highlanders were sent from Darien to Fort Moosa, a few miles from St. Augustine. There, in June 1740, they were attacked by five hundred Spaniards and Indians. Only twenty-six Highlanders survived, and only a few of those survivors elected to return to Darien. The Spaniards felt confident that Darien was effectively destroyed. However, another group of Highlanders arrived from Scotland the following year, prompting Oglethorpe to declare that "the Darien settlement flourishes exceedingly."

The Highlanders had the final say. The men from Darien extracted their revenge, put an end to Spanish aggression in Georgia, and earned a place in history in July 1742 at the Battle of Bloody Marsh. (For more information about the "War of Jenkins Ear" and the Battle of Bloody Marsh, see The Marshes of Glynn Tour, pages 134–35.) After the conflict, the military post at Darien was no longer necessary. The Highlanders turned their energies to the planting of rice, sugar, and indigo.

In the early 1800s, Darien became a commercial center. In 1823, fire raged through the city and did extensive damage. The next year, a hurricane nearly washed away the rice fields. Despite these setbacks, the city remained a world leader in cotton exports until 1845.

During the Civil War, Federal troops looted and burned most of the city's offices, warehouses, and wharves. After the war, Darien found a new prosperity in the timber business. By 1868, Darien lumbermen were shipping more than 20 million board feet of yellow pine each year. It was said that a person could walk for miles on the timber rafts on the river and never get his feet wet.

Begin your tour of town at Fort Darien, located near the welcome center. This fort was built in 1736, six months after the landing of the first Scottish Highlanders. You can also walk down the steps to the river and view the tabby ruins of buildings erected from 1810 to 1830, during Darien's reign as a major commercial port. These are the buildings that were destroyed by Federal troops in 1863.

From the welcome center, drive one block on Fort King George Drive and turn left on Franklin Street. Travel one block to Vernon Square.

Laid out in 1806, Vernon Square is listed on the National Register of Historic Places. The square was organized according to the same concept of town planning James Oglethorpe practiced in Savannah. Throughout the nineteenth century, Vernon Square was the business, cultural, social, and religious

Saint Andrews Episcopal Church

Tabby ruins at Darien waterfront

center of Darien. Churches, banks, and homes of leading merchants were built around the square. Many of the old homes and churches still stand.

One of the churches is St. Andrews Episcopal Church, chartered in 1843. In 1844, a large wooden building with a belfry was built near this site. This original church was burned by Federal troops in 1863. The present structure, copied from an English church, was completed in 1878.

Darien United Methodist Church

On the opposite side of the square stands Darien United Methodist Church, organized in 1836. It, too, was set afire by Federal troops, but when it did not burn completely, it became the rallying site for the rebuilding of Darien. What the Yankees couldn't do, a hurricane completed in 1881. The current sanctuary was built in 1883.

After viewing Vernon Square, return to Fort King George Drive and turn left to see St. Cyprian's Episcopal Church, ahead on the right. St. Cyprian's was constructed in 1876 by former slaves, many of whom had worked on nearby Butler Island. It was built for "the Colored People of McIntosh County" and named for an African bishop who was an early martyr. The church suffered severe damage during a hurricane in 1896, but it has since been restored.

St. Cyprian's Episcopal Church

Continue on Fort King George Drive for 1 mile to the Fort King George Historic Site. Begin your tour of the fort at the museum. From the museum, you can walk to the cemetery, where the unknown soldiers are buried. The historic site features a replica of the original blockhouse built by Tuscarora Jack Barnwell. You can also see reconstructed earthworks and the fort itself.

Please note that the historic site is closed on Mondays.

Return to the welcome center and turn right on U.S. 17. After three blocks, turn left on Third Street West and drive two blocks to Darien Presbyterian Church.

The first Presbyterian church in the colony was established by the Scottish Highlanders in 1736. From that time, Darien became the center of Presbyterianism in Georgia. The first Presbyterian church in Darien was built in 1808. It later burned. In 1876, it was replaced by a new church on the present site. That building was destroyed by fire in 1899. The present Victorian Gothic chapel dates from 1900.

Return to U.S. 17. In the small square at the intersection of Third Street, U.S. 17, and GA 99, you will see the Highlander Monument, a memorial to the original Scottish settlers.

Follow GA 99 for 1.4 miles. Turn right at the sign for St. Andrews Cemetery. It is one block on this unpaved road to a plot of ground overlooking the marsh. This cemetery was established for the Spalding family in 1818.

Perhaps best remembered for being among the first to plant sea-island cotton in coastal Georgia, the Spaldings had deep roots throughout this area. James Spalding was an early landowner and a well-to-do trader on St. Simons Island. A descendant of the Spaldings of County Perth, Scotland, he was heir to the Barony of Ashantilly. His wife, Margery McIntosh Spalding, was a

Darien Presbyterian Church

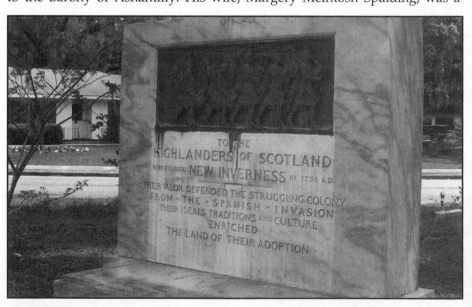

Highlander Monument

descendant of the clan that settled Darien in 1736.

Ashantilly

Their son, Thomas Spalding, purchased a large tract of land on Sapelo Island in 1802, at age twenty-eight. Although his home on Sapelo is much more extravagant, he built a structure in Darien as the family's home on the mainland, christening it Ashantilly, after the Spaldings' ancestral home in Scotland. Thomas Spalding was a stalwart believer in tabby construction. He was born in a tabby home, and he died in the tabby Ashantilly. He built quarters for his slaves out of tabby. Family members who preceded him in death were laid to rest in tabby tombs. Ironically, his own tomb is brick.

Thomas Spalding wore many hats, including those of planter, writer, and statesman. He was a leading proponent of experimental agriculture, publishing many articles on the subject, and one of the first coastal planters to practice crop rotation.

His agricultural interests began with a desire to become a vintner. This venture failed miserably, with Spalding only managing to make one pipe of wine. A great believer in fortified beverages, he added ten to fifteen gallons of brandy to that single pipe.

Next, he took up long-staple cotton. He was awarded a trophy in England for an essay he wrote about the introduction of sea-island cotton, or black-seed cotton, in the United States. Sea-island cotton thrived best in sandy soil near salt water. Distinguished by its black seeds and silky fibers, sea-island cotton was carefully bred so that its fiber length increased from one year to the next. This variety was so popular that many planters didn't even send their cotton to market. French lace mills contracted for it before the seed was even planted.

Cotton plantations were slow in coming to the coast, even though many knew the crop would do well here. Rice and indigo commanded a better price. After the Revolution, the English encouraged the East India Company to cultivate indigo, and the English markets turned away from America. In response, coastal planters began to change from indigo to cotton. With the invention of the cotton gin, cotton became more economical to produce. By the early decades of the nineteenth century, Georgia and South Carolina were producing most of the cotton marketed in the United States. Men with large numbers of slaves bought out small landholders. During a four-month period in 1815, an estimated 10,259 bales of sea-island cotton were shipped out of Savannah. Three years later, that number jumped to 61,797 bales.

Many planters began plowing their profits into buying more slaves and more land to place under cultivation. Although his wealth lay in cotton, Thomas Spalding was one of the few who perceived that sole reliance on this crop could be devastating.

Spalding struggled with the issue of slavery. Though opposed to it in principle, he saw it as necessary to his own agricultural enterprises and the economic well-being of coastal Georgia in general. By all accounts, he was humane in the treatment of his slaves. He built a tabby home for each family and provided garden plots so they could raise their own vegetables.

Spalding's overseer was a famous slave known as Ben-Ali, the Mohammedan. Legend says he was born to royalty in the French Sudan. Although his fellow slaves understood little of his native dialect, Ben-Ali spoke both French and English fluently.

One story is told of how Ben-Ali beat off a party of invading British during the War of 1812. Thomas Spalding armed a group of his slaves, an unheard-of practice at the time. Under Ben-Ali's leadership, the group of black soldiers stole through the heavy undergrowth and routed the British landing party.

Through the years, Thomas Spalding became known as the elder statesman of Georgia. He was elected president of the Georgia Convention in 1850, when rumblings of secession were just beginning. He steered the convention on a course that kept Georgia in the union. He was quoted as saying that the preservation of the United States was "an appropriate termination of my long life." Spalding died in 1851, so he never had to witness the dissolution of the country he loved so dearly.

From the cemetery entrance, turn north onto another unpaved road. It is a short distance to where the tabby Ashantilly mansion is visible on the left. It is 0.3 mile on this road to another unnamed road. Turn left again. After one block, turn right on GA 99, heading toward Meridian.

It is 1.1 miles to The Ridge, a place of lovely old Victorian homes built by local bar pilots and timber barons during Darien's heyday as a timber-exporting port. One of the quaintest villages on the Georgia coast, The Ridge is listed on the National Register of Historic Places. Many of the homes have striking ornamental gingerbread trim on their porches. Almost every house has delicate filigree ornamentation. A story is told of the owner of one of the most ornate houses at The Ridge, who decided to move to St. Simons Island. Rather than leave his house, he had it taken down, each piece labeled, and the entire structure reassembled on St. Simons.

Continue 4 miles to the town of Meridian. If you have made ferry reservations and purchased your ticket, follow the clearly marked signs directing you to Sapelo Dock Road. The ferry dock is 0.7 mile off the highway.

Sapelo Island, like St. Catherines and Ossabaw islands, was given to Mary

Musgrove and used by the Creek Indians for hunting, bathing, and fishing. In 1760, Sapelo and Ossabaw were sold back to England. (For more information about Mary Musgrove Bosomworth and the treaty which gave these lands to the Native Americans, see The Signers Tour, page 97.)

In the years that followed, Sapelo Island changed hands several times. One owner was a French aristocrat named Francis Dumoussay Delavauxe. He sold parts of the island to other Frenchmen, two of whom lived the rest of their lives at an estate called Le Chatelet. The slaves had difficulty pronouncing the French, so they changed the name to "Chocolat."

There was a chef at Le Chatelet named Cupidon. Legend says he frequently searched the island for truffles on behalf of his master, who loved the delicacy from his native land. Cupidon employed the same method used even today in France to find the mushrooms—he led a pig on a leash through the forest. The delicacy grows underground, and pigs can smell it and root it out.

Houses at The Ridge

When Thomas Spalding purchased the island, he and his wife, Sarah, designed and built a mansion on the south end of the island. They called it South End House. The house was built low to the ground to withstand hurricane winds. The columns were recessed, and the house was constructed of hand-hewn beams. The tabby walls that Spalding admired so much were three feet thick. Sarah Spalding died in 1843, after which Thomas continued living in the mansion until his death in 1851. At that point, the plantation

The ferry to Sapelo Island

passed to his young grandson.

In 1861, Confederate troops set up defenses on Sapelo Island, and the Spalding family evacuated. After the war, they returned to find their home in ruins.

They did, however, have a reunion with their former nanny, Betsy Beagle, who welcomed them back with open arms. Betsy lived to the age of ninety-four. Upon her death, the Spaldings erected a marker that read, "In memory of Betsy Beagle, she was the faithful loving nurse of the Spalding children for two generations. 'My Baba,' may she rest as peacefully as the little heads she pillowed to sleep on her bosom."

Although cotton was still grown on the island, Thomas Spalding's old predictions started to come true. Continuous cotton planting was sapping the soil's strength. Fertilizers were too expensive. And to top it off, the boll weevil arrived in Georgia. Soon, this insect destroyed much of the cotton crop.

As the economic structure of the area changed, so did the title to the land. Like many coastal plantations, Sapelo Island was now worth more as a hunting preserve for wealthy industrialists than as an agricultural enterprise. There were few better places to hunt than abandoned rice fields on the Atlantic Flyway that attracted millions of ducks each season. Men such as Bernard Baruch, Isaac E. Emerson (the inventor of Bromo-Seltzer), and Marshall Field and families with names like Hutton, Luce, and Vanderbilt began finding their way to the South Carolina and Georgia coasts.

In 1925, Howard Coffin, the founder of Detroit's Hudson Motors, bought the island. The Spaldings' house had already been partially renovated as a place for sportsmen, but Coffin refurbished it as his vacation retreat. In 1925, the Coffins enlarged the house. They soon entertained many famous guests. In 1928, President and Mrs. Calvin Coolidge joined the Coffins for Christmas. Charles Lindbergh came soon after his transatlantic flight.

After Mrs. Coffin's death in 1932, Sapelo was sold to R. J. Reynolds, Jr., popularly known as "Dick" Reynolds. The son of the famous North Carolina tobacco magnate, Reynolds was interested in Thomas Spalding's agricultural experiments. He also spent time visiting the homesteads of the descendants of Spalding's former slaves.

Many of these descendants lived in an area called Hog Hammock, named for Samuel Hog, the hog minder for the Spaldings. His descendants still live in the community today, but they have changed their name to Hall.

After emancipation, the Spalding family deeded its former slaves the plots of land they had worked during slavery. This community evolved into Hog

Hog Hammock Community Center

Hammock. Today, except for the portion belonging to the residents of Hog Hammock, Sapelo Island is owned by the state; the people of Hog Hammock are the only private landowners on the island.

The schoolhouse that Reynolds built for the residents is now a community center. The children travel to school by ferry to the mainland. They are bused to the dock, ferried across the water, and then bused to school. The entire trip takes about an hour. If you come on a weekday for the 8:30 A.M. island tour, you will probably see the children coming to the mainland for school.

The average age of the residents of Hog Hammock is sixty-five. Although many have clear title to their land, a stipulation in many of the deeds rules that the state has first refusal rights on the property if they decide to sell.

Your tour of the island begins with a thirty-minute ferry ride. After arriving on the island, you will board a tram with a tour guide. One of the first things you will see is the airstrip built by Dick Reynolds. Wild turkeys and deer eat the growth around the airstrip, effectively keeping it mowed. The Sapelo deer herds are large, but the deer themselves are small. Their size is believed to be due to genetic dwarfism, likely the result of the inbreeding necessitated by their isolation.

The tour meanders through tropical foliage to Behavior Cemetery, built by the Spaldings in the early 1800s. It was named Behavior to encourage good conduct among the plantation workers. Some of the grave markers are hand-carved and obviously very old. The oldest stone in the cemetery marks the resting place of a person born in 1784.

Burials on the island are more complicated than those on higher ground. As the highest elevation on the island is twelve feet above sea level, water has to be pumped out of the hole for a few days after a grave is dug.

The next landmark on the tour is a large house situated among the trees. When Howard Coffin owned the island, he had several aunts who wanted to live here, too. Unfortunately, they did not get along with each other well enough to live in one house, so Coffin built them two identical homes. This is one of them.

One of the houses built by Howard Coffin for one of his aunts

The tram makes a stop at Long Tabby. Before restoring South End House, Coffin built Long Tabby as a temporary residence for his family. The family lived here from 1912 to 1922. After they moved to the main house, Long Tabby was used as a guesthouse and later as a vacation retreat for underprivileged boys.

Artifacts are on display in Long Tabby. Among them is the cranium of a loggerhead sea turtle believed to be between fifty and seventy-five years old.

Ruins of Thomas Spaulding's sugar mill

St. Lukes Baptist Church

B. J. Confectionery

An endangered species, the loggerhead has to be thirty-five years old to reproduce, at which time the female lays between 100 and 150 eggs in a nest near the ocean. Sixty-four loggerhead nests were counted on the island in 1992. Although turtle eggs are protected against human interference, raccoons eat some of them. When the turtles hatch, the babies frantically make their way toward the ocean. During this migration, the raccoons often wait for their feast. The researchers on the island don't interfere with the raccoons because their habits are part of nature's process. However, they will quickly interfere when humans intrude.

Adjacent to Long Tabby are the tabby ruins of the Spalding sugar mill, built in 1803. Thomas Spalding was the first Georgia planter to cultivate sugar cane. The grinding stones in this mill were propelled by animal power. This area offers a good view of the waterways surrounding the island.

The next stop on the tour is Hog Hammock. There, you can see St. Lukes Baptist Church, which boasts a congregation well over a hundred years old. St. Lukes shares a minister with the island's other church, First African Baptist Church; the minister comes by boat on Sunday mornings. On the fifth Sunday of the month, family members who live on the mainland come over on a special run of the ferry to have dinner on the grounds after the service.

The older members of the congregation remember a time when it took a lot to become a member at St. Lukes. In order to become a member, one had to have a dream. The dream had to be "approved" by the family, then by the deacons. If the dream was not considered heartfelt, the person was not accepted as a member. Old traditions die hard on Sapelo Island. The men still sit on one side of St. Lukes and the women and children on the other.

The tour makes a stop at B. J. Confectionery, a store operated by Viola Johnson. Items for sale range from peppermint candy in old-time jars to bird nests. Photographs of President and Mrs. Jimmy Carter attest to the fact that they were visitors at the store while he was governor of Georgia and later president.

The next site is the horse and cattle complex built by Dick Reynolds. Reynolds hired a German contractor to construct a road connecting the complex to the main house. The family envisioned a road that curved under a canopy of moss-draped oaks. When they returned from a European vacation, they found an open, straight road. Reynolds fired the man and threw him off the island. However, he did name the road "The Autobahn" in honor of the unfortunate contractor's German roots.

The complex looks like an European village. Elaborate buildings face a

Horse and cattle complex

The turkey that sits atop the fountain built by R. J. Reynolds, Jr.

courtyard, where the focal point is a fountain in the shape of a turkey. Wild turkeys are abundant on the island even today. Reynolds was intrigued by them and built the fountain as a gift for his wife. She was not amused. Legend has it that she took a loaded gun and shot at the turkey on the fountain.

There is a museum in the complex. One of its highlights is a collection of preserved snakes, including a "coachwhip snake." Old-timers will tell you that a coachwhip snake can put its tail in its mouth and transform itself into a hoop. The hoop then rolls through the woods or down a roadway and catches its victim. Then the snake straightens itself, wraps around the victim, and crushes him or her to death.

Reynolds used the barn in the complex as a movie theater, where he showed first-run movies to his guests. One of his guests supposedly quipped that Sapelo Island was a good place to be a cow.

A lighthouse stands on the shore of Sapelo Island, but it is not currently part of the tour. You can, however, see it from the tram while riding to the main house. The state has purchased the land, and plans are under way to eventually open it for the public.

During a hurricane in 1898, waves destroyed the houses on the eastern end of the island and killed most of the livestock. In the course of that storm, the

South End House

TOURING THE COASTAL GEORGIA BACKROADS

foundation of the lighthouse cracked. The keeper was investigating the crack when he noticed members of his family being washed out to sea. He swam out and pulled them to shore one by one.

The main attraction of the tour is unquestionably South End House. When Reynolds bought the property, he added a children's wing to the renovations undertaken by Howard Coffin. All the fixtures in that wing are small, designed to accommodate children's hands. There is a "Circus Room" on the top floor; the ceiling looks like a tent, and clowns and wild animals are painted on the walls. On the darker side, the infamous kidnapping of the Lindbergh baby so worried Reynolds that he had barred windows installed in the children's wing.

The huge basement of South End House contains a bowling alley. In front of the house is a reflecting pool filled by water from an artesian well. The statues in and around the pool were crafted in Florence, Italy.

Near the house is a trail that winds through the dunes to Nanny Goat Beach. At low tide, the strand seems to be a mile wide, and sand dollars and whelks are everywhere. Visitors are asked to check the seashells they plan to take with them to make sure there are no animals alive inside!

If you take the all-day tour of Sapelo Island, one of the stops is Le Chatelet. The ruins of that estate can still be seen.

Today, South End House is used as a conference center by the University of Georgia. It is open to nonprofit groups. Visitors stay in the house's thirteen bedrooms while attending conferences. There is talk that South End House will eventually be turned into a museum only. Sapelo Island is also home to the University of Georgia Marine Institute.

Across the sound to the north of Sapelo is Blackbeard Island, named for the legendary pirate. Supposedly, this was one of Blackbeard's many coastal hideouts. For many years, Blackbeard Island was considered part of Sapelo. Later, it came under the ownership of the United States Navy, which hoped to use the island's live oak timber for constructing ships of war, though it apparently never followed through on that plan. Today, Blackbeard Island is a National Wildlife Refuge accessible only by water. The beach is open to the public during daylight hours, if you can arrange transportation.

After your tour of Sapelo Island, return to GA 99 in Meridien. Continue in your original direction on GA 99. It is 8 miles from Meridien to U.S. 17. Turn right on U.S. 17, heading north. Drive 2.2 miles to Pine Harbor Road. Turn right. After 0.1 mile, turn left on Shellman Bluff Road. It is 6.7 miles to Shellman Bluff, one of the most picturesque villages on the coast of Georgia. All the lanes on the

Shellman Bluff

*Harris Neck National
Wildlife Refuge*

TOURING THE COASTAL GEORGIA BACKROADS

left lead to the Broro River. You can take any one of them until you reach a cliff. There, you will find cottages with gorgeous views of the river, marshes, and marinas. A narrow, unnamed road leading along the top of the cliff offers an exceptional view; this road is popular among pedestrians as well as motorists.

After viewing Shellman Bluff, backtrack 2.6 miles on Shellman Bluff Road to Young Man Road and turn right. After 4.2 miles, turn right on Harris Neck Road. It is 1.9 miles to the entrance to Harris Neck National Wildlife Refuge, on the left. Here, piers and docks jut into the marshes to allow visitors to enjoy picnicking, photography, fishing, crabbing, and wildlife observation; visitors can also launch their boats. The park contains 2,687 acres of grassland, forest, salt marsh, and fresh water. Within the park, there are over 15 miles of roads open to hiking.

"Smallest Church in Georgia"

It is another 0.8 mile on Harris Neck Road to an unpaved road on the left. Follow this unpaved road for 0.5 mile to Barbour River Landing, a scenic place on the Swain River. Armadillos are abundant in this area. You will often see the bodies of unlucky members of this species that have been hit by cars.

In times gone by, the most famous part-time resident of Harris Neck was New York tobacco manufacturer Pierre Lorillard. One day in the 1880s, Lorillard was cruising down the inland waterway in his yacht when he noticed a particular piece of Georgia land that seemed ideally suited as a place of quiet and privacy for a second home. Beginning in 1891, he constructed a lavish estate at Harris Neck.

Retrace your route to Harris Neck Road and turn right. It is 7.4 miles through forests of oak, pine, and yucca to U.S. 17. Turn north.

Interior of
"The Smallest Church in Georgia"

It is 0.1 mile to a church which is so small it appears to be a child's playhouse. In fact, the sign indicates that it is "The Smallest Church in Georgia." Coastal residents have made a local landmark of this church. They are quite fond of showing it off to relatives and visitors.

Located on U.S. 17 and convenient to nearby I-95, this church was built for travelers, and its register suggests that it serves that purpose well. For being so close to such well-traveled thoroughfares, it is a surprisingly restful place, nestled in a grove of pine trees. The interior has a high-pitched roof with exposed beams. The lancet windows are stained glass. The aisle leading to the altar runs between two rows of six chairs.

The tour ends here, at Georgia's smallest church. It is 1.2 miles farther along U.S. 17 to Exit 12 off I-95.

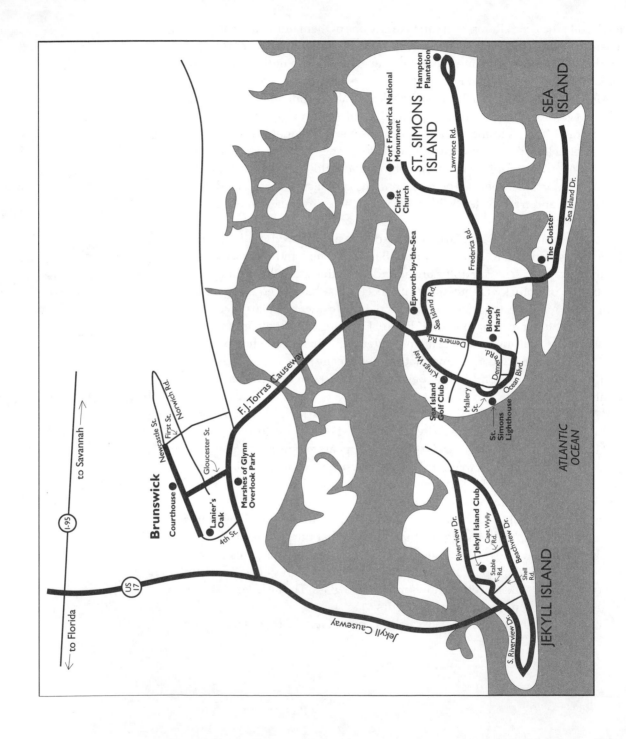

The Marshes of Glynn Tour

This tour begins in Brunswick and travels to St. Simons and Sea islands. It ends with a tour of Jekyll Island.

Total mileage: approximately 72 miles.

Brunswick is reached via U.S. 17 some 18 miles south of Darien or via the Golden Isles Parkway, which is Exit 8 off I-95. The tour of Brunswick begins at Lanier's Oak, located in the median of U.S. 17 South some 0.4 mile south of the F. J. Torras Causeway.

Captain Mark Carr arrived in Georgia in 1738. The following year, he was granted five hundred acres on the present site of Brunswick. There, he developed a fine plantation that produced corn and tobacco, among other staples. What is now the city of Brunswick was first known as Carr's Fields.

Carr quickly distinguished himself in military matters, commanding a marine company and helping turn back an invasion by the Spanish in 1742. When it was proposed that a town be laid out on the site of his plantation, Carr willingly relinquished his land in exchange for a tract on Blythe Island, where he then made his home.

The new town was christened Brunswick in 1771 in honor of the British royal family, who were of the House of Brunswick. When the streets and squares of the port village were laid out, names such as Newcastle, Norwich, Prince, and Gloucester gave Brunswick a decidedly English flavor.

That sentiment changed during the Revolutionary War. Glynn County, of which Brunswick is the county seat, was one of Georgia's eight original counties organized under the state constitution in 1777. It was named in honor of John Glynn, a member of the British House of Commons who had defended the cause of the American colonies prior to the Revolution.

Brunswick was abandoned during the war, but business returned afterward. It was made a port of entry in 1789, and eight years later, it was chosen the county seat. The town continued in a boom-bust cycle for decades until it was finally incorporated in 1836. In 1837, the Oglethorpe House, Brunswick's first hotel, was opened. It was an elegant establishment, its groaning board laden with fish from the sea and oysters and shrimp from the marshes.

As residents of a port city, the people of Brunswick have always been proud of their boats. This pride reached its peak in the early part of the nineteenth century, when Brunswick natives took it upon themselves to try to prove to Northerners that they had the mechanical skill and imagination to construct boats that could beat any Northern-made vessel.

In 1837, the members of the Aquatic Club of Georgia ran an offer in New York newspapers challenging any of the New York clubs to meet them in competition. Months went by, and there were no takers. The Georgians would not give up their fight. They next approached the boating club at Augusta, just up the Savannah River. The Augusta club had recently purchased some New York-made boats that had won races on the Hudson River. The Aquatic Club challenged the Augusta club to enter their "Whitehall wherries" against Brunswick's canoe boats. But even the Augusta club would not rise to the challenge.

This refusal came as a severe disappointment to the gentlemen of the Aquatic Club. Nonetheless, they decided to make the best of the situation by holding their regatta as scheduled, on January 16, 1838, though it would not be the hoped-for contest between Northern and Southern boats.

On the appointed day, thousands of spectators lined the shore for the social event of the season. In the first race, the *Devil's Darning Needle*, owned by Richard Floyd of Camden County, defeated the *Goddess of Liberty*, owned by Henry duBignon of Jekyll Island. Boats from Glynn and Camden counties appeared in a variety of races. It was a memorable day of elegance and fellowship. According to Burnette Vanstory in *Georgia's Land of the Golden Isles*, one boat, a green-colored craft called the *Lizard*, "was thought too slippery a customer and was not allowed even to creep over the race course." It was all in good fun.

In the 1850s, the Brunswick and Altamaha Canal opened, and construction started on a railroad to Brunswick. But then came the Civil War. In May 1861, Camp Semmes beckoned young men to join the Confederate forces, and the Brunswick Riflemen were organized. In 1862, the Federals blockaded the coast, and Brunswick was evacuated. Just before the town was occupied by Federal troops, Oglethorpe House was accidentally burned.

Brunswick lay dormant during the postwar years and an epidemic of yellow fever in 1876. However, it revived in the 1880s, when the area became a center for the timber industry. Dry docks, lumbermills, a foundry, and turpentine stills took their places along the waterfront. Oglethorpe House was replaced by the Oglethorpe Hotel, and L'Ariosos Opera House was built. Another yellow fever epidemic struck in 1893.

With the coming of World War I, ships and barges brought newcomers to the port of Brunswick. In 1924, St. Simons Island was connected to Brunswick and the mainland by the F. J. Torras Causeway, an event that eventually opened the area to tourism.

World War II brought feverish activity to coastal Georgia and the Brunswick area in particular. The early years of the war were difficult on coastal shipping, with German U-boats sinking unescorted merchant vessels almost at will. In early 1942, the oil tanker *Oklahoma* met such a fate off Brunswick. Many local residents saw the ship's burned hull towed into port or even met some of the fifty-four survivors when they were brought to safety on St. Simons Island. It was the first of many such incidents off the Golden Isles.

In response, the government chose Brunswick as the site for the Glynco Naval Air Station, informally known as the "Blimp Base." Construction began in the summer of 1942. The site, 6 miles north of town, was chosen because of its proximity to the ocean and because of the absence of air obstructions in the area. The massive project presented engineers with some unusual difficulties. A blimp storage facility requires huge buildings, yet construction steel was in short supply throughout the war, and Georgia hurricanes are notorious for their lack of kindness to man-made structures. It was with some trepidation that construction proceeded on the station's two hangars, the largest wooden structures in the world at that time. Amazingly, the hangars stood for twenty-seven years before they fell to Hurricane Dora. The structures were 1,000 feet long, 297 feet wide, and 150 feet high. Old photographs reveal that each could accommodate six blimps simultaneously.

Ideally suited for anti-submarine reconnaissance, blimps were part of the strategy for protecting shipping along the coast. The usual practice was for three blimps to fly ahead of a shipping convoy, many of which included a hundred or more vessels, to look for U-boats. Supposedly, blimps from the Glynco base escorted ninety-eight thousand ships by the close of the war and did not lose a single one to submarine attack.

The Glynco facility continued to play a variety of air-related military roles for many years after World War II. In recent years, its function has shifted to ground-based law enforcement. Today, it is the home of the Federal Law Enforcement Training Center.

But the biggest wartime operation in Brunswick was the yard where Liberty

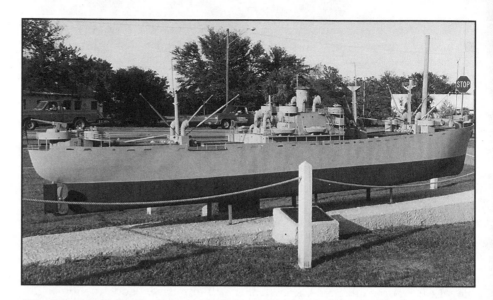

A replica of the City of Brunswick, *one of the Liberty ships*

ships were built by the J. A. Jones Construction Company of Charlotte, North Carolina. Liberty ships were small cargo vessels, typically 416 feet long and weighing 10,500 tons. The war effort called for a great number of such vessels to be built as quickly as possible. The goal was to have each Liberty ship completed within 105 days of the time it was begun.

Toward that end, the J. A. Jones Construction Company hired local residents in great numbers and trained them from scratch. At its peak, the shipyard employed sixteen thousand men and women and had a weekly payroll of over $1 million. More than seven thousand housing units had to be built in Brunswick and on St. Simons to accommodate the workers. Eleven miles of railroad track were laid on the 435-acre site.

The *James M. Wayne*, the first Liberty ship produced by the yard, enjoyed a successful career, making runs to Europe and Africa. The *William B. Woods*, the yard's second ship, was not so lucky. It was hit by a torpedo in the Mediterranean in 1944. Thirty of its crew survived by clinging to mattresses, but the remainder perished with the ship. The yard produced a total of ninety-nine Liberty ships. During its best month, it launched seven ships, delivered seven others, and laid keels for another seven.

One of the newcomers brought to Brunswick by the shipbuilding industry was Captain Alfred Henson. His wife, Elizabeth, wrote about one of the favorite entertainments for Brunswick ladies in those years—the "Coca-Cola Party." Ladies would assemble between eleven and noon at the home of the hostess. Trays of tall, iced glasses filled with Coca-Cola were passed, followed by platters of crackers and small cakes. Other bottled drinks were usually provided for ladies who did not like Coca-Cola, but those were few in Brunswick. Invented in Atlanta in the 1880s, Coca-Cola was by then a Georgia favorite. This simple, inexpensive form of entertainment was particularly popular with young women wanting to honor a visitor or an upcoming bride.

Lanier's Oak, where this tour begins, is the oak where Sidney Lanier took in the breathtaking view across the vast tidal marshlands and was moved to pen his famed "Marshes of Glynn," considered a masterpiece of nineteenth-century American poetry. In the poem, Lanier wrote,

> Ye marshes, how candid and simple
> and nothing-withholding and free
> Ye publish yourselves to the sky and
> offer yourselves to the sea?

Lanier's Oak

Lanier was born in Macon. He had just graduated from Oglethorpe University and was planning to do graduate work in Germany when the Civil War broke out. He joined the Confederate forces. By the end of the war, he had spent four years in a Union prison. His health in ruins and his fortune gone, he came to Brunswick to visit relatives and try to regain his strength. He spent many hours under this large oak viewing the marshes that stretch "leisurely off, in a pleasant plain, to the eternal blue of the main."

In the years after the war, Lanier studied law and worked as a hotel clerk. A gentleman of varied talents, he was called "the Sir Galahad among our American poets" by author T. W. Higginson. His best-known poems include "Sunrise," "Song of the Chattahoochee," "An Evening Song," and "A Ballad of Trees and the Master." A self-educated musician, Lanier was also considered by some to be the greatest flute virtuoso of his time. He lived in Baltimore toward the end of his life, performing with the Peabody Orchestra and lecturing on English literature at Johns Hopkins. He died in 1881.

Marshes of Glynn Overlook Park

From the oak, head south on U.S. 17 for 0.2 mile to Marshes of Glynn Overlook Park, on the left. This park provides a fantastic view of "the world of marsh that borders a world of sea." The marshes, now protected by law, provide an important buffer between the ocean and the mainland. They prevent erosion and provide a rich spawning ground for shrimp and other marine life.

On the opposite side of U.S. 17 is Gloucester Street. Follow Gloucester Street through a business district for 0.9 mile to the red-brick city hall, on the right.

Victorian houses in Brunswick

The shrimp fleet at Brunswick dock

At city hall, turn left on Union Street, which is part of the historic area called "Old Town." This divided street boasts some of the loveliest old homes in town. After eight blocks, make a loop around the median and continue back to Gloucester on the other side of Union Street.

Turn left on Gloucester. After 0.2 mile, cross Bay Street to the block-long waterfront park which runs between Gloucester and F streets. This park affords visitors a place to walk and take in the Brunswick shrimp fleet. Brunswick is considered one of the shrimp capitals of the world. The best time to view the fleet is late afternoon.

After you have enjoyed the park, follow F Street for three blocks to Union Street and turn left. Continue one block to the "Old Courthouse," erected in 1902. The Old Courthouse is nestled among moss-draped oaks and palmettos, as well as more exotic specimens like tung trees and Chinese pistachio trees.

When you arrive at the Old Courthouse, you are facing G Street. Turn left on G Street and continue two blocks to Newcastle Street. Turn left and travel four blocks to a red-brick building with a tower. This is "Old City Hall."

Continue on Newcastle for five blocks to Prince Street. Turn left and drive nine blocks to Albany Street. Prince Street is a divided thoroughfare lined with Victorian houses; trees meet overhead. A stroll down any of the side streets is recommended. Turn left on Albany and drive 0.6 mile to Gloucester Street. Turn right. Continue 0.6 mile to U.S. 17. Turn left. It is 0.5 mile to the F. J. Torras Causeway. Turn right just before the causeway and stop at the local visitor center. In the garden is a replica of the *City of Brunswick*, one of the Liberty ships built here during World War II.

After leaving the visitor center, follow the causeway across the Mackay River, which is part of the Intracoastal Waterway; you will have to pay a modest toll. The 4.3-mile causeway also crosses the Frederica River.

The causeway marks the entrance to St. Simons Island and Sea Island, part of the chain of coastal islands known as the Golden Isles. In the 1500s, gold-seeking Spanish explorers called these islands golden because of their lustrous, sandy beaches, natural beauty, and glorious weather.

The first inhabitants of St. Simons Island were the Guale Indians. In the seventeenth century, Spanish Jesuit missionaries based in St. Augustine, Florida, attempted to convert these Native Americans to Christianity. The Spanish established three missions on what they called Isla de Asao. The main mission, called Asao by the Indians and San Simon by the Spanish, eventually lent its name to the entire island. After several bloody uprisings, the Jesuits withdrew. They were replaced by Franciscan missionaries. The Franciscans

Brunswick's Old Courthouse

Brunswick's Old City Hall

did not have any better luck and were finally forced to leave.

Soon after the founding of Savannah, James Oglethorpe selected St. Simons as the best position for a frontal defense against the Spanish. In 1734, his forces began construction of a fort on the island's western flank near a bend in the river. The river, the fort, and the settlement that sprang up around it were named Frederica in honor of the prince of Wales. The fort built to guard the island's southern tip was known as Fort St. Simons.

The village surrounding Fort Frederica began with forty-four men and seventy-two women and children in March 1736. It eventually grew into a community of approximately a thousand. As the settlement expanded, temporary huts were replaced by brick and tabby dwellings.

By all accounts, Frederica was a bustling place, with red-coated British regulars patrolling the streets alongside kilted Scottish Highlanders. (For more information about the Highlanders, see The Planters Tour, pages 111–12.) James Oglethorpe himself maintained a large farm and home nearby, which he called Orange Hall. Later, James Spalding and his family lived in this home. Referred to as "the General's Farm" during Spalding's ownership, this home was the birthplace of Thomas Spalding. The exact location of Orange Hall is not known.

In the late 1730s, England and Spain came into conflict during what has been called the "War of Jenkins Ear." This strange name was born when Spanish soldiers captured the brig *Rebecca* and cut off the ear of a British citizen named Jenkins. The English had designs on Spain's territory, and this was just the excuse they needed to mount an attack.

Oglethorpe organized a strong expeditionary force that sailed straight into the harbor at St. Augustine. The English sacked the town, but the coquina-walled Castilla de San Marcos was invulnerable to their cannons, so Oglethorpe withdrew.

In 1742, the Spanish retaliated with a landing on St. Simons Island. They then sent two detachments to find the best approach to Frederica. Oglethorpe's forces attacked the Spanish as they marched single file down a narrow trail in a dense forest. Many were killed, and the rest fled.

The Spanish returned with reinforcements, but the Georgia forces were nowhere to be found. They were actually hiding near a huge, open marsh on St. Simons. When the Spanish reached the marsh, they believed themselves safe and began cooking their dinner. Out of the marsh came Oglethorpe's troops, and the Battle of Bloody Marsh was under way. Oglethorpe's force of seven hundred men was smaller than that of the invaders, but upon losing some of their key officers, the Spanish withdrew, never to threaten Georgia again. With the Spanish threat overcome, the garrison at Frederica was withdrawn and the town abandoned.

The island regained importance during the Revolutionary War and the War of 1812 for its rock-hard island oaks. These massive live oaks were used in building the warships of that era, including the USS *Constitution*, better known as "Old Ironsides."

In 1772, James Spalding began a large plantation on the land formerly owned by Oglethorpe. A supporter of England, he left the island during the Revolution. When he returned, his home and farm were in ruins.

But the Spalding family bounced back by being among the first to cultivate coastal Georgia's newest crop, sea-island cotton. Since this crop could only be grown on the narrow islands along the coasts of South Carolina and Georgia, a powerful caste of plantation owners quickly developed. By the early 1800s, these planters had built luxurious homes on St. Simons. Although these homes were sacked by the British during the War of 1812, the planters' wealth enabled them to quickly rebuild.

The end of the Civil War did not leave them so well off, and it was only with the establishment of several sawmills in the 1870s that the island's economy began to recover.

As the twentieth century approached, St. Simons became a popular summer vacation resort. Guests were transported by a pair of steamships until the causeway opened in 1924. The new road made the island more accessible, but careful planning has kept development to a tasteful level.

After crossing the causeway, turn left on Sea Island Road and drive 0.1 mile to Hamilton Road. Turn left and proceed 0.1 mile to Arthur J. Moore Drive. Gascoigne Point is located across the intersection. The Guale Indians had one of their villages on this bluff.

Captain James Gascoigne was the man who brought Oglethorpe's first settlers to Frederica in 1736. He later established a plantation on the bluff that now bears his name.

Gascoigne Point is the location of Epworth-by-the-Sea, a Methodist conference center named in honor of the British birthplace of John and Charles Wesley.

After one of his trips to England, James Oglethorpe brought along two Anglican missionaries—John and Charles Wesley—to minister to the spiritual needs of his settlers in Georgia. By 1736, the Wesleys had established a church on St. Simons.

It soon became apparent that Charles Wesley and James Oglethorpe had different goals for the Georgia settlement. Oglethorpe's main interest was establishing a barrier against Spanish expansion. He felt this could best be accomplished by building stable communities protected by fortifications. Wesley, on the other hand, was intent on his evangelical mission. He regarded all other business as subordinate to the business of the church. This obviously created some differences of opinions. Charles was the Anglican cleric for Fort Frederica for several months in 1736. When he began to feel that his mission was impossible, he departed for England.

After his brother's departure, John Wesley returned to Frederica four times before leaving "with an utter despair of doing good there," as he put it. The victim of an affair of the heart, John eventually returned to England like his brother before him. (For more information about John Wesley's activities in America, see The Tybee Light Tour, pages 67–68.)

John Wesley went on to found the Methodist church in Great Britain and America. Charles Wesley remains best known for the more than six thousand hymns he wrote.

In later years, the area around Gascoigne Point became part of the sea-island cotton plantation of James Hamilton. The wharf built at the point became the shipping center for all the plantations on the island. From 1874 to 1902, the bluff was lined with sawmills.

Finally, in 1949, the South Georgia Conference of the Methodist church purchased the old Hamilton property and converted it to a conference center and religious retreat. With one of the Wesleys' first churches on St. Simons, it is appropriate that this site was chosen for Epworth-by-the-Sea. Today, the facility includes a dining room that can serve six hundred people, a prayer tower, auditoriums that can seat sixteen hundred, and the Arthur J. Moore Methodist Museum, the largest museum of Methodist history in the country. As you enter the museum, you are greeted by a larger-than-life statue of John Wesley. A video and dioramas depict the Wesleys' landing in Georgia and their mission to the natives. The grounds also include Lovely Lane Chapel, built in 1880 and named for Lovely Lane Church in Baltimore, the site of the founding conference of American Methodism.

Statue of John Wesley at the Arthur J. Moore Methodist Museum

When you leave Epworth-by-the-Sea, return to Sea Island Road and turn left. Proceed 2.5 miles to Frederica Road and turn left again. After 0.3 mile, turn left on Atlantic Drive. Continue 0.7 mile to land's end. The water beyond the end of Atlantic Drive is Dunbar Creek, which flows from the Frederica River. The house on the left at the end of the road is located on the former site of Ebo Landing.

According to a record at the Library of Congress, a ship bearing slaves from the Ebo tribe of Africa landed here one morning many years ago. The slaves made their way off the vessel slowly, as they were secured at the ankles by rings of iron. Once ashore, they took in their surroundings. They looked at one another, and without saying anything, they turned and walked together toward the water, slowly, restrained by their shackles. Once they set foot in the water, their pace slackened even more. At sunset, they could still be seen in the distance. They never looked back. Supposedly, someone watching from shore offered the simple observation, "They're going home." The next morning, there was no trace of them.

When his home was under construction, the current owner of the property found a tabby cornerstone from a slave-era building.

The Ebo Landing site continues to be of considerable interest to historians, writers, and African-Americans. Several years ago, the head of the Ebo tribe of Africa even paid a visit to this historic spot on Atlantic Drive.

Lovely Lane Chapel

Retrace your route to Frederica Road and turn left. After 2.7 miles on Frederica Road, you will see Christ Church on the left. Facing the road at the entrance to the churchyard is the Wesley Oak. This huge tree offered a canopy of shade for John and Charles Wesley when they held services on this site well before the construction of the present church.

Christ Church

After viewing the oak, stroll to the gabled, white frame church. In 1808, a hundred acres of land near the town of Frederica were granted to a group of citizens who wanted to build a church. The land was rented out and the proceeds used to pay construction fees. Christ Church was built in 1820. It was confiscated by Union troops during the Civil War and nearly destroyed. In 1889, it was rebuilt by Anson Phelps Dodge, Jr., in memory of his first wife, Ellen, who had died during their round-the-world honeymoon. Dodge eventually became rector of the church. Among his life's accomplishments were the establishment of endowments for the church and a boys' home and the establishment of a fund to support missionaries.

The church building is of cruciform design with a trussed Gothic roof. The stained-glass windows commemorate incidents in the life of Christ and the early history of the church on St. Simons.

The adjacent graveyard contains the grave of Anson Phelps Dodge, Jr., as well as those of Howard Coffin and his wife. (More information about Howard Coffin is presented later in this tour.)

This graveyard is also home to one of the island's ghosts. Over the years, many people have seen a light flickering among the old tombstones. Legends say it's the ghost of a young woman who was so afraid of the dark that she molded hundreds of beeswax candles and always kept her home ablaze with light after sunset. Following her death, her husband began to worry about his wife's tomb sitting in the dark. One night, he left a lighted candle at her grave. This soon became a nightly ritual, one he continued until his death. There are those who say you can still see the lights shining in the old graveyard, though the sightings have become rarer since the cemetery was enclosed by a brick wall.

Continue on Frederica Road. It is 0.2 mile to the entrance of Fort Frederica National Monument.

What the Spanish invasion could not destroy, time has. Today, there is little left of either the fort or the town. The museum on the premises offers a film about the fort's past. Visitors can also stroll on what used to be Broad Street in the town of Frederica, which adjoined the fort. Archeological excavations in the 1950s confirmed the locations of palisades, walls, and buildings. Earthworks have been partially reconstructed. The tabby powder magazine still overlooks the Frederica River. The foundations of other shops and dwellings have been excavated. Conveniently placed placards describe the original structures and their probable use.

After viewing the remains of the fort and village, return to Frederica Road,

turn right, backtrack 0.9 mile to Lawrence Road, and turn left. Drive through heavily wooded former plantations for 4.9 miles to Hampton Point. Bear left on Butler Lake Drive. You are now entering the former Hampton Plantation.

In 1774, Major Pierce Butler purchased this land and Little St. Simons Island, located across the Hampton River. He turned the area into one of the most efficient plantations in the South. It took almost two decades to complete the "Big House," the formal gardens, and the various outbuildings, but by the late 1700s, Hampton had become one of the most prestigious plantations on the Georgia coast.

Burnette Vanstory commented on Pierce Butler in *Georgia's Land of the Golden Isles*:

> The major, austere and dignified autocrat that he was, differed in every way from his easy-going neighbors; and the strict military regulations and discipline at Hampton were in marked contrast to the leisurely atmosphere of the other plantations. . . . The casual visitor arriving by boat must state his name and business to a warden . . . before being escorted to the Big House. Managed with the regimental efficiency that was part of Pierce Butler's nature, Hampton was a model community that produced everything needed in the daily life of its inhabitants.

In 1804, Vice President Aaron Burr's long-running feud with Alexander

Hamilton ended in what is probably America's most famous duel. Hamilton, likely a future president, was mortally wounded, and Burr, fearing both legal prosecution and public opinion, fled south. He came to Hampton Plantation, where he was welcomed by his friend Pierce Butler.

Burr found St. Simons Island and Hampton Plantation to be an excellent escape, both literally and figuratively. Local people were generally pleased to have so eminent a person among them, regardless of his offense. During his stay, Burr wrote his daughter that Hampton "affords plenty of milk, cream and butter; turkeys, fowls, kids, pigs, geese and mutton; fish of course in abundance; figs, peaches, melons, oranges and pomegranates."

In 1839, the plantation passed to Pierce Butler II, the husband of famous actress Fanny Kemble. The time she spent at Hampton Plantation is part of Fanny's classic book, *Journal of a Residence on a Georgian Plantation, 1838–39.* (For more information on Pierce Butler, Pierce Butler II, and Fanny Kemble, see The Planters Tour, pages 107–8.)

Pierce and Fanny's daughter Sally inherited Hampton Plantation, which eventually passed to her son, novelist Owen Wister. Pierce and Fanny's daughter Frances inherited neighboring Little St. Simons Island, which was eventually sold to a pencil manufacturer in the early 1900s. That company harvested the island's abundant red cedar trees. For many years after that, the island was left in its natural state. Since World War II, the rustic "Inn on Little

Ruins of the Hampton Plantation manor house

St. Simons" has offered guests some of the most naturalistic lodgings imaginable. It can accommodate up to twenty overnight guests.

Continue on Butler Lake Drive for 1.3 miles to McBride Street. Turn right. Go one block and turn left on Pierce Butler Drive. It is 0.2 mile to Hampton Point Drive, which circles through an elite residential area. You can see Little St. Simons Island in the distance. Little St. Simons can be reached only by boat.

Turn left on Hampton Point Drive. After one block, you will see the tabby ruins of the old slave quarters at Hampton Plantation. Turn around and head in the opposite direction on Hampton Point Drive. After 0.1 mile, you will see the tabby ruins of the Hampton Plantation manor house. The ruins are nestled among modern residences but are still clearly evident.

Tabby ruins of the slave quarters at Hampton Plantation

Continue on Hampton Point Drive 1.5 miles to Lawrence Road. Turn left. After 4.9 miles, the name changes to Frederica Road. Continue 2.2 miles on Frederica to Sea Island Drive. Turn left and travel 1.7 miles. You will leave St. Simons Island and travel to Sea Island at this point.

After crossing Village Creek, you will soon see signs for The Cloister. Turn left to enter the grounds of one of the finest hotels in the country.

In 1910, Howard Coffin, the builder of the Hudson and Essex automobiles, came to Savannah to attend an auto race. He liked Georgia so much that he decided to invest in it. His first purchase was Sapelo Island in 1911. For the next

The Cloister

thirteen years, he divided his attention between his Dayton, Ohio, company and his island off the coast of Georgia.

When Coffin was still an infant, his father had died, and he had then been raised by his relatives, the Jones family. Years later, when his cousin Alfred Jones, Sr., became ill with tuberculosis, Coffin invited him to recuperate on Sapelo Island. Jones visited the island and subsequently became one of Coffin's closest advisors there.

In 1926, Coffin and some fellow investors purchased Sea Island, originally known as Long Island, as a hunting preserve. The island was richly endowed with native deer and turkeys. Coffin also stocked it with pheasants. Hunting parties began frequenting the island on what they called "maroons," camping in tents on the beach during their trips.

Coffin came up with the idea of building a grand hotel on St. Simons Island. Alfred Jones, Sr., was one of the primary men who convinced him to build it on Sea Island instead. Jones also suggested that the hotel should not be grand, but a simple, comfortable overnight inn.

Coffin found his architect in Addison Mizner, who was noted for his villas in Palm Beach, Florida. A twenty-three-year-old graduate of Ohio State University, T. Miesse Baumgardner, oversaw the landscaping—no small feat, since the area chosen for the inn was part marsh and part goat pasture and in bad need of dredging.

On October 12, 1928, an excited group of locals, many of whom had invested in the hotel, held a private celebration for the opening of what was billed as Coffin's "friendly little hotel." The official opening, with four hundred specially invited guests, followed on October 27.

Today, The Cloister is still friendly, but it is certainly not little. The resort includes a colony of cottages, privately owned residences, and a Mobil five-star hotel. A beach club and a gun club are on the premises, and horseback riding, fine dining, and numerous other activities are available for guests and residents.

After seeing The Cloister, you can take a side trip to enjoy the exclusive homes in the residential portion of the island; Sea Island Drive, the main road on the island, stretches north for thirty-five blocks.

After you have enjoyed Sea Island, retrace your route to Frederica Road on St. Simons Island and turn left. Drive 1.9 miles to Demere Road. Turn left. It is 0.5 mile to a parking lot from which you can view Bloody Marsh. The precise site where the famous battle took place is not known.

Continue 0.6 mile on Demere and turn left on East Beach Causeway, where

Marker at the site of the Battle of Bloody Marsh

you will again have an excellent view of Bloody Marsh. Continue 0.4 mile to Ocean Boulevard and turn right. Go 0.4 mile to Massengale Park, located on the left. This beach area offers several miles of public access.

Continue 1 mile on Ocean Boulevard to Twelfth Street. Turn left, go two blocks, and turn right. The St. Simons Lighthouse is on your left.

In the 1730s, James Oglethorpe built Fort St. Simons to protect the southern tip of the island from Spanish invasion. Oglethorpe spiked the guns at the fort prior to the Battle of Bloody Marsh.

In the opening years of the nineteenth century, John Couper purchased the former site of the fort and renamed it Couper's Point. In 1804, he sold the land to the government for one dollar so a lighthouse could be built on it.

During the Civil War, Confederate troops constructed Fort Brown on the property containing the original lighthouse. The fort was abandoned in 1862, at which time the Confederates blew up the lighthouse to prevent its use by Federal troops.

The present lighthouse was constructed in 1872. Originally powered by kerosene, it has been powered by electricity since 1934. It is one of only five light towers in Georgia today. The light from its original third-order Fresnel lens is visible 18 miles out to sea.

It seems like every lighthouse has its ghost, and the St. Simons Lighthouse

St Simons Lighthouse

is no exception. Tradition has it that the spirit of a slain keeper paces up and down the spiral steps night after night. It is said that the footsteps always stop just short of the uppermost landing and just before the ground-floor landing.

One keeper and his family who lived here for twenty-five years were often fooled by the footsteps. The wife would hear steps coming down the stairs and put dinner on the table, but no one would come in. Likewise, the keeper would often think his wife was coming up to visit, but she wouldn't appear.

In 1971, the keeper's dwelling was converted to a museum designed to preserve the history of coastal Georgia. The exhibit is managed by the Coastal Georgia Historical Society. If they have the stamina, visitors are welcome to climb the 129 steps to the top of the lighthouse for a magnificent view of the area.

After viewing the lighthouse, retrace your route to Ocean Boulevard and turn left. Drive 0.6 mile to Retreat Avenue; Ocean Boulevard changes to Kings Way en route. Turn left onto Retreat Avenue and drive under the oaks to Sea Island Golf Club.

Thomas Spalding, who owned Sapelo Island before Howard Coffin, also owned Retreat Plantation, formerly located here. Spalding built a replica of Orange Hall, the home where he was born, at Retreat. (For more information about Thomas Spalding, see The Planters Tour, pages 114–16.)

Spalding sold Retreat to William Page. Page's daughter, Ann Matilda Page, married Thomas Butler King, who served in the Georgia Senate and later in the United States Congress. With her husband in Washington much of the time, Ann Matilda became a cotton planter and developed a prosperous plantation.

The Kings divided their time in Georgia between Retreat and their mainland plantation, Waverly, located near Kingsland. While on St. Simons, they stayed in a homey English cottage with a gabled roof and a shuttered veranda. They also set out rows of oaks—the same avenue of oaks which greets visitors approaching Sea Island Golf Club today.

In 1926, Howard Coffin purchased Retreat and converted the property to a golf course. Thankfully, his Sea Island Company adopted a policy of preserving historical landmarks by developing around them. Today, the old corn barn from Retreat Plantation forms the nucleus of the golf course's clubhouse. You can see the tabby ruins of the plantation at the end of the drive, just beyond the parking lot. The old cemetery where the plantation slaves were buried, the ruins of the old slave hospital, and the chimney of the "Big House," which burned, are all visible on the property.

After viewing the remains of Retreat, return to Kings Way and turn left.

Ruins of the "Big House" at Retreat Plantation

Ruins of the old slave hospital at Retreat Plantation

Drive 1.3 miles to New Sea Island Road and turn right. Continue 0.2 mile to a traffic light and turn left on the F. J. Torras Causeway. After traveling the 4.4 miles across the causeway, you will find yourself back on the mainland at U.S. 17.

Turn south on U.S. 17. After 4.2 miles, turn left at the Jekyll Island sign. It is a 6.3-mile trip across the Jekyll Island Causeway; en route, you may wish to stop at the welcome center, located on the left. As you enter Jekyll Island, you will need to stop at the ticket office, located in the median, to pay a modest toll for driving on the island.

Continue 0.1 mile past the ticket office to the first left-turn lane. Make a U-turn and proceed 0.1 mile back toward the ticket office. Turn right on North Riverview Drive.

Jekyll Island is the smallest of the Golden Isles. Its original Indian settlers called it Ospo. It was later claimed by Spain, which sent missionaries in the late sixteenth and early seventeenth centuries. Santiago de Ocone, the Spanish mission on Jekyll, vanished when hostile Indians and pirates took over the island. By 1733, when James Oglethorpe established the first permanent Georgia settlement in Savannah, nearly all traces of the Guale Indians and the Spanish mission had disappeared from Jekyll.

In 1734, Oglethorpe passed the island on one of his southern expeditions. He named it for Sir Joseph Jekyll, one of Georgia's financial sponsors. William Horton, one of Oglethorpe's most trusted officers, soon cleared fields on Jekyll and planted grain and hops for use in the production of beer for the troops at Frederica. The Spanish destroyed this plantation as they crossed the island on their retreat after the Battle of Bloody Marsh. Not easily discouraged, Horton rebuilt his home, and by 1746, the plantation was fully restored.

Horton's son inherited the Jekyll Island property in 1749. The son showed little interest in the property, and the island was sold at public auction for nonpayment of taxes several times before being purchased by Christophe Poulain duBignon.

Christophe was a much-decorated French naval captain whose loyalty to Louis XVI during the French Revolution forced him to flee his native Brittany. With four other French Royalists, he purchased Sapelo Island and then Jekyll Island. By 1794, he had enlarged William Horton's house and made it his own. He planted sea-island cotton and lived the life of a prosperous planter until his death in 1825. The island empire he built encompassed eleven thousand acres. His parties were legendary, and everyone in colonial high society sought an invitation to his estate.

Christophe's son Henri continued to plant cotton. It was during his ownership that the *Wanderer* put in at Jekyll Island carrying the last major cargo of slaves ever sent to the United States.

A fundamental change took place on the coast of the southeastern United States after the Civil War. On one hand, the war destroyed the plantation system from which the aristocracy had profited so well. On the other hand, rich Northerners were beginning to seek warm locations in which they could escape the bitter winters. Former plantations appealed to them as perfect places to hunt ducks, deer, wild turkeys, quail, and other wildlife, and the old manor houses could easily be converted to comfortable hunting lodges.

It isn't surprising, then, that John Eugene duBignon and his brother-in-law Newton S. Finney conceived the idea of selling Jekyll Island to a New York club as a private hunting retreat. As a member of the Union Club, a meeting place for wealthy, influential men, duBignon was in an ideal position to negotiate the sale. A price of $125,000 was agreed upon—quite a jump from the $13,100 duBignon had spent acquiring the island less than six months earlier. On January 8, 1886, the Jekyll Island Club was officially incorporated. The club was supposed to have a limit of a hundred shares of stock, but demand was so great that the charter list had to be expanded. Indeed, the membership

The Jekyll Island Club

View from Jekyll Island Club

register read like a who's who of late-nineteenth-century America, featuring such names as Morgan, Vanderbilt, Astor, Gould, Rockefeller, Armour, Goodyear, Pulitzer, and Macy. Membership was passed on by inheritance, and the privacy of the island's residents was jealously guarded.

On April 4, 1886, the *New York Times* announced that "the Jekyl [*sic*] Island Club is going to be the 'swell' club, the *creme de la creme* of all, inasmuch as many of the members are intending to erect cottages and make it their Winter Newport."

The first of these "cottages," begun in 1888, was the property of McEvers Bayard Brown, a reclusive New York banker. Brown built the home for his bride-to-be, but she subsequently broke off their engagement, and the lovelorn millionaire refused to live in his new cottage. Never occupied, the Brown House was torn down years later. Brown's eccentricities continued after he left Jekyll Island. He took up residence in England and kept a yacht off the coast. He maintained a complete crew and provisions aboard the boat in case he ever needed to sail on short notice. This yacht was never used either.

The surviving cottages of Jekyll Island are visible on the right after about 0.6 mile on North Riverview Drive. They are mansions by most people's standards. Many of them are now owned by the state of Georgia, due largely to the efforts of a former governor, Melvin E. Thompson. Following the death of Governor-elect Eugene Talmadge shortly before his inauguration in 1947, Lieutenant Governor Thompson found himself thrust into the governorship until the next election. It was during this term that he moved the state to acquire Jekyll Island for $675,000. The year-round resort has since become one of Georgia's greatest assets.

The first cottage along this row is Moss Cottage. William Struthers, head of a Philadelphia marble firm, built this home in 1896.

Next is the Goodyear Cottage. This many-gabled white house was built by Walter Rogers Furness, an architect and member of an old Philadelphia family. In 1896, he sold the house to Joseph Pulitzer, who later sold it to the Goodyear family.

The next house is Mistletoe Cottage, built in 1900 by Henry Kirk Porter. The gray shingles in this house are the original ones, made of cypress. Cypress is called "the everlasting wood," and the appearance of the shingles here gives credence to that description. An interesting aspect of this house is the large bathrooms. One of them is even large enough for twin tubs.

Next comes Indian Mound, also known as the McKay-Rockefeller Cottage. It was built in 1892 by Gordon McKay, an inventor and shoe-machinery

Mistletoe Cottage

manufacturer. William Rockefeller purchased it in 1904 and made extensive renovations. It now has 8 bedrooms and 11½ baths. Supposedly, McKay's wife was the daughter of a servant. Not long after she married McKay, she divorced him and married a German diplomat. It must have been an amicable divorce, because McKay gave the couple $100,000 as a wedding gift.

Past Indian Mound, the road curves to the right to the Jekyll Island Club. Weather permitting, you might see people dressed in "proper attire" playing serious croquet on the lawn.

Visitors are encouraged to visit the club and have lunch. Inside, you can still dine in the Grand Dining Room. Since most of the millionaires took all their meals here, some of the cottages have small, almost inadequate kitchens.

The Victorian clubhouse has not only been the domain of some of America's most influential people. One day in 1899, it also played host to what could have been a major political deal. President William McKinley and most of his administration arrived in Brunswick on five of the most luxurious cars the railroad could furnish. From there, they traveled by steamer to Jekyll Island, where they met with Speaker of the House Thomas Reed to decide who should be the next president of the United States. Senator Mark Hanna, one of the most influential political leaders of the day, played moderator.

Patrol boats prowled the waters to keep the press from getting wind of the secret meeting, but a young reporter for the *Brunswick News*, L. J. Leavy, learned of the proceedings and wired the story around the country. Leavy's mysterious source was an unnamed, socially prominent, cigarette-smoking female who had granted him an interview on a private railway car. The national press was initially skeptical of the story, but once its authenticity was verified, it was reported nationwide. The "Millionaire's Club" on Jekyll Island hardly fit the image of a smoke-filled room, anyway. The deal was off.

Drive under the porte-cochere and go behind the clubhouse. There, you will see the duBignon Cottage. Though this wooden structure is rather plain by the millionaires' standards, it holds the distinction of being the first cottage on Jekyll Island to have a kitchen.

Turn right on Old Plantation Road. The J. P. Morgan Tennis Court building, constructed in 1929, is on the left. After 0.2 mile, turn left on Stable Road. The Museum Orientation Center is located on the right after a short distance. The island offers a tram tour that includes visits inside some of the famous cottages; the tour leaves from the Museum Orientation Center. This building once served as the stable for the Jekyll Island Club.

Continue on Stable Road for 0.7 mile and turn left on Old Plantation Road.

DuBignon Cottage

Crane Cottage

TOURING THE COASTAL GEORGIA BACKROADS

It is 0.3 mile to Faith Chapel. This small chapel has a Tiffany stained-glass window. While the church was under construction in 1904, Louis Comfort Tiffany came to Jekyll Island and personally supervised the installation of the window.

Old Plantation Road intersects North Riverview Drive just before Faith Chapel; turn onto North Riverview. You will pass along the side of the Crane Cottage as North Riverview heads directly toward Jekyll Creek, then along its front as the road turns north and runs parallel to the creek. This cottage is the largest private structure ever built on the island. Richard Teller Crane, Jr., was a manufacturer of bathroom fixtures. It is not so surprising, then, that his house has seventeen bathrooms. It also has an enormous kitchen, unlike many of the other cottages.

On the right beyond Crane Cottage are two decorative lions. These are nearly all that is left of Chichota, a cottage constructed by D. H. King, Jr., in 1897 and sold to Edwin Gould in 1900.

The house next door is Hollybourne, otherwise known as the Charles Maurice Cottage. Maurice was an engineer and a pioneer builder of iron and steel bridges. This tabby house was constructed in 1890.

Continue on North Riverview. After 2.6 miles, you will see the ruins of Georgia's first brewery on the left. This is the site where beer was brewed for the troops at Fort Frederica. You can still see the large pieces of tabby where the brewery stood.

The remains of William Horton's home are located 0.1 mile farther on North Riverview Drive; this house was later used by the duBignon family. Across the road from the ruins is the duBignon burial ground. Christophe Poulain duBignon was buried here with a live oak tree as his monument.

Continue on North Riverview for a 10-mile tour of the entire perimeter of the island. The name of the road changes to North Beachview Drive as you round the northern tip of the island and begin heading south along the ocean. It then changes to South Beachview Drive, then to South Riverview Drive as you round the southern tip and begin heading back north. The tour ends at the intersection of South Riverview and the Ben Fortson Parkway. Turn left to leave the island.

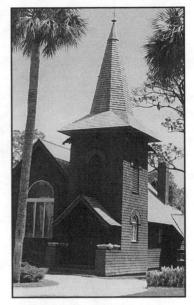

Faith Chapel

Ruins of Georgia's first brewery

Ruins of Horton House

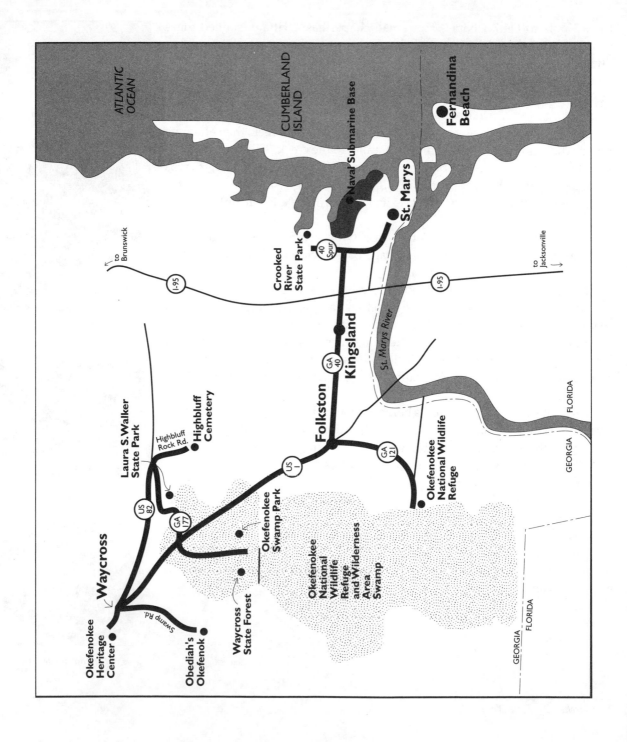

The Swamp to Sea Tour

This tour begins northwest of Waycross at the Okefenokee Heritage Center, then visits downtown Waycross before heading to Obediah's Okefenok. It travels to High Bluff Cemetery, Okefenokee Swamp Park, and the Okefenokee National Wildlife Refuge, then visits Kingsland. A walking tour of historic St. Marys follows. The tour ends with a boat trip to Cumberland Island.

Total mileage: approximately 142 miles.

The tour begins at the Okefenokee Heritage Center, located on North Augusta Avenue approximately 2.5 miles northwest of Waycross. If you are approaching from U.S. 82, head north on North Augusta; if you are approaching from the north on U.S. 1, head west on North Augusta. The heritage center provides a good introduction to the unique culture of the Okefenokee Swamp.

The swamp was once part of the ocean floor. It was formed as an entrapped depression when the land around it rose out of the sea during the Pleistocene age nearly a million years ago. The Okefenokee lies in a basin 120 feet above sea level. Tannic acid released by decaying vegetation gives the water its characteristic black color; the locals say it looks like tea brewed strong enough

Okefenokee Swamp

to straighten a horseshoe. Cypress trees are another characteristic feature of the swamp. Cypress knees, so popular in the making of lamps, jut from the roots out of the water.

Okefenokee is an Indian name that means "Land of the Trembling Earth." The name describes the vast peat beds and floating islands that shook underneath the feet of the Indians but nonetheless supported great forests and entire tribal villages. The Indians considered the swamp magical, and indeed, it still lends itself to such an interpretation. Its vast silences are unbroken except for the cries of water birds and the sounds of fish falling back into the black water after jumping into the air. The swamp is home to over five thousand American alligators and a multitude of reptiles, fish, and bears. Arrowheads four thousand years old are sometimes found underfoot.

Residents of the Okefenokee have always been an independent people, living off the land and water by hunting and fishing. The turpentine trade brought a living to the people of the swamp during the Depression. Turpentine was, in effect, the sea-island cotton of the Okefenokee. The trade has all but died out today.

When the Okefenokee was designated a wildlife refuge in 1937, many of the old swamp families were pushed out of the region. Still, poachers were taking alligator hides from the swamp as late as the 1960s. And of course, moonshine was made in the swamp until the penalties were toughened. These lifestyles remain in the blood of some people of the Okefenokee. The sound of distant gunfire can still be heard at night; men still hunt deer with packs of dogs on the sly. Other residents are content to work at the paper mill at nearby St. Marys.

The museum at the Okefenokee Heritage Center offers exhibits highlighting the life of people in and around the swamp. Indian culture and local history are documented through artifacts and displays. Art exhibits are also featured.

Other exhibits are located outside. Prominent among them are a 1912 Baldwin steam locomotive, a tender, and additional railroad cars. Western Union facilities from a long-ago era are housed in a train-station building. A few feet away is a building containing a print-shop exhibit of the *Waycross Journal* of bygone days. Nearby is the Thomas Hilliard House, an 1840s farmhouse complete with outbuildings. Just walking up the crude wooden steps and sniffing the musty smell so characteristic of old houses will transport you back in time.

Make sure you also visit Southern Forest World, located next to the Okefenokee Heritage Center. Southern Forest World is a private, nonprofit interpretive center that tells the fascinating story of Southern forestry. Visitors

1912 Baldwin Steam locomotive at Okefenokee Heritage Center

Southern Forest World

can study the naval-stores operations of yesterday and today, learn what managing a forest means, see a collection of old logging tools, walk inside a giant loblolly pine, and see a mummified dog in a tree.

When you are ready to leave, turn left on Augusta Avenue, heading south. After 1.4 miles, turn left on Carswell Avenue. Follow Carswell 1.7 miles to Pendleton Street. Turn right. It is one block to Waycross City Hall.

Since its earliest days, Waycross has been known as the place where stagecoach roads and pioneer trails converged in southern Georgia. Later, the Brunswick Railroad and Western Railroad lines crossed here, giving birth to a modern rail network. Even today, all the roads in this part of the state seem to lead to Waycross. Former Indian trails, coach roads, and military trails have been developed into modern highways, some of them following the routes laid out by local pioneers such as Major Harry Haines, superintendent of the Savannah Railroad; Daniel Lott, a founder of Waycross; and B. F. Allen, editor of the *Georgian*. Indeed, the name of the town signifies that it is a place where "ways cross."

Waycross was formed in 1872 and incorporated in 1874. Local cotton production was almost wiped out by the boll weevil, and some of the forests in the area were leveled by careless actions. Nonetheless, progress has been steady through most of this century. Formerly known as a sawmill, turpentine, and farming town, Waycross has developed into an industrial and tourist center. It is promoted as "the Largest City, in the Largest County, in the Largest State east of the Mississippi." It is also known as the entrance to the Okefenokee Swamp.

What is now Waycross City Hall was originally the Young Men's Christian Association Center. The building was designed by Henry John Klutho, an architect whose work was inspired by Frank Lloyd Wright. Many of Klutho's admirers consider this to be among his finest work.

Waycross City Hall

The city of Waycross acquired the "Y" in 1917 and added a new cornerstone at the northeast corner of the building. In 1982, architects analyzed the structure to determine whether it could be renovated to suit the city's needs. It could. Work on the exterior included cleaning, painting, repairing brick-work and woodwork, adding a small plaza with a flagpole on the Pendleton Street side, and planting cherry and Chinese elm trees. The interior moldings and trim in the first-floor lobby spaces were restored, and a skylight well in the second-floor lobby was reopened and rebuilt. It was well worth the effort. Today, Waycross City Hall is a beautiful building.

Continue south two blocks to where Pendleton Street ends at Plant Avenue. This is a good place to leave your car if you would like to visit the two small parks located just to your left.

The first park was built to honor the Confederate dead. Its monument is made of white marble.

Just beyond this park and across Elizabeth Street is Doughboy Park. At its center is the bronze Doughboy Monument, dedicated to the memory of "our comrades who entered the service from Ware County and gave their lives in World War I." Sponsored by the local American Legion post, it was erected in 1935. Another monument in the park boasts an eternal flame; this monument is dedicated to the men who served in World War I, World War II, the Korean War, and the Vietnam War. Visitors enjoy Doughboy Park for its comfortable benches and scenic landscaping. The large, brick gazebo constructed in the mid-1980s is another popular spot.

Opposite the two parks is the old Waycross Railroad Station, now used as offices.

Turn right off Pendleton Street onto Plant Avenue. After one block, turn left onto Jenkins Street. Cross the railroad tracks, continue one block, and turn right on Haines Street. The King Edward Cigar factory will soon appear on the right.

Doughboy Park

Monument to Confederate dead

Old Waycross Railroad Station

In 1861, David S. Swisher, a merchant in Newark, Ohio, accepted title to a small cigar factory in what was soon to become Waycross in payment of a debt. In this simple, almost accidental way, the foundation was laid for an enterprise that has grown into one of the largest of its kind in the world.

The now-famous King Edward brand did not come into the company's line until 1918. In that year, Swisher's company purchased the rights to the label from a merchant it had been packing privately branded cigars for. A King Edward cigar originally cost ten cents. Even at that lofty price, it enjoyed a steadily rising popularity. During the 1920s, the economics of greater production made it possible to reduce the price to five cents. During the Depression, when the price was further reduced to two for five cents, sales went sky-high. As a result, the company was able to continue its plant expansion and add hundreds of new employees even during those dark days.

Plant enlargements have continued steadily since that time. The factory currently produces more than three million cigars daily. As the company's president, Tim Mann, put it, "In addition to being a dominant manufacturer of cigars in the United States, we are this country's largest exporter of cigars. Our products are shipped to over 60 nations and, through licensing agreements, are made in several countries around the world."

Employees of the King Edward Cigar factory are justifiably proud of their company's history. Tours of the facilities are offered five days a week.

Continue south on Haines Street. After 0.6 mile, the road changes to Brunel Street. Another 0.7 mile later, the name changes to Swamp Road. Continue 6.8 miles to Obediah's Okefenok, the 1800s homestead of Obediah Barber. En route, you will see a variety of country homes, a huge pecan grove, and lovely wooded areas.

Obediah's Okefenok

Obediah Barber was born on July 25, 1825. He and his father, Isaac, were the first white settlers on the northern border of the Okefenokee Swamp. At the age of six, Obediah assisted his father and the state surveyors in determining a boundary line between the state of Georgia and the territory of Florida. A natural botanist and zoologist, he developed a great love for the plants and animals of the Okefenokee. However, he is best remembered for his physical strength. One day, the six-foot-six Obediah was out tending his livestock when he found himself under attack by a huge black bear. Unarmed, he grabbed a piece of wood and bludgeoned the bear into submission. This and other such feats of bravery earned him the moniker "King of the Okefenokee." Others called him the "Southeast Paul Bunyan."

Obediah married three times and fathered twenty children by his first two wives. He distinguished himself during the Civil War by supplying the Confederate army with meat from his herd of cattle. He died in 1909 at the age of eighty-four.

The centerpiece of Obediah's Okefenok is the cabin constructed by Obediah Barber in the mid-1800s. Also on the property are a sugar cane mill, a smokehouse, a gristmill, a blacksmith shop, a turpentine shed, and a moonshine still, as well as nature trails, animal exhibits, and a general store. Together, these facilities offer a look into the Okefenokee Swamp's past and a good recreational outing for the entire family.

From Obediah's Okefenok, retrace your route to the King Edward Cigar factory. Continue on Haines Street beyond the factory; after a block and a half, the name changes to Screven Avenue. After another 0.3 mile, Screven feeds into U.S. 1. Continue 1 mile to U.S. 82, also known as the Brunswick Highway. Head east on U.S. 82. After approximately 8.7 miles, turn right on Highbluff Rock Road. Follow this road for 1.1 miles to High Bluff Cemetery, located on the right.

High Bluff Cemetery is best known as the resting place of Lydia Stone Crews. Lydia was one of the five daughters of William and Sarah Smith, who came to the Okefenokee Swamp around 1836. Two of the Smith girls were of normal size, while the other three were considered giantesses, standing at least six-foot-two. Red-haired Lydia, born in 1864, was one of the big girls. She

The gravestones of Lydia Stone Crews and her family

became known during her lifetime as the "Queen of the Okefenokee." Not to be outdone, one of her oversized sisters moved to Florida's Everglades and was called the "Ox Woman."

Lydia was both a hard worker and an astute businesswoman. She rode herd on six hundred cattle, oversaw a bunkhouse of male cowhands and plowmen, and was a major landowner in the area. She once explained the origin of her wealth this way: "When I was a girl, my pappy gave me and my sisters a cow and a sow apiece and told us if we would look after 'em we could make some money. Before the year was out, I made a few dollars off'n mine and had saved every penny of hit. After anuther year I made 'nough to buy 45 acres of land. I got hit dirt cheap." Some of her land was purchased at less than a dollar an acre.

It wasn't long before she increased her holdings to 3,000 acres. In 1903, she married Gordon Stone, one of her hired hands. Unfortunately, Stone was as shy and sickly as Lydia was outgoing and vigorous. Stone died in 1926, by which time Lydia had accumulated some 39,000 acres of timberland.

She soon married again. Lydia was by that time sixty-three, while her new husband, J. Melton Crews, another hired hand, was only twenty-one. Lydia wore a hand-beaded white wedding dress that had been three months in the making, but it did little to take off her rough edges. She called her new husband "Doll Baby" and paid him this high compliment: "His plowing was straight; his crossties were the correct length and weight; and he knew how to face a b'ar." Doll Baby most likely felt right at home with Lydia, whose kitchen contained a stuffed bear she had killed herself.

Doll Baby's violent streak, it turned out, ran deeper than just "facing b'ar." One day, a neighbor, Layton Hendrix, came to Lydia's house for unknown reasons, and Doll Baby shot him. Though Doll Baby claimed he mistook Hendrix for a burglar, the fact that Hendrix was allowed to bleed to death without medical attention did little for his case. He was convicted of murder and sentenced to twenty years at hard labor. Lydia first paid a restaurant to provide meals for her chain-gang husband, then decided she wanted him out of prison altogether. She traveled to Atlanta and paid a public official a $25,000 bribe for his release. Such was her influence that when she got back home and stopped payment on the check, her husband stayed free.

It is said that during the Depression, the banks in Waycross were closed to everyone but Lydia. When she came to town to close out her account, she brought a revolver rather than a passbook.

When Lydia learned she was dying of cancer, she expressed the wish that

Doll Baby marry another red-haired woman. Together, they arranged such a marriage before her death in 1945. By that time, Doll Baby was a good catch— Lydia left him half a million dollars and timber and turpentine businesses worth much more than that.

Interest in Lydia Stone Crews continued well after her death. In 1973, a son of Bing Crosby came to Waycross to make a movie of her life. Unfortunately, that movie never came to pass.

Today, visitors can see Lydia's grave in High Bluff Cemetery. Her monument is one of several standing in a group, all of them over six feet tall. The others mark the graves of Lydia's parents, Gordon Stone, Doll Baby Crews, and Nancy Smith, another of Crews's wives. If you look closely, you'll be able to identify Lydia's marker with little trouble. Hers stands slightly taller than the rest, much as she did in life.

When you are ready to leave the cemetery, retrace your route to U.S. 82 and turn left. Drive 1.4 miles, then turn left on GA 177 at the sign for Laura S. Walker State Park. It is 2 miles to the park.

Laura S. Walker State Park

Laura Singleton Walker was a teacher, a writer, a civic leader, and a tireless campaigner for conservation. Her husband was a beloved physician. During her lifetime, Laura Walker earned a couple of unusual distinctions—she became both the only living person and the only woman for whom a Georgia government park is named. The park came into being through the agency of Senators Richard Russell and Walter George during the administration of Franklin Roosevelt. Today, a large lake at the park provides facilities for swimming, canoeing, water skiing, and other sports. The swimming pool on the premises is also popular. Major facilities include forty-four tent and trailer sites, a group camp, picnic shelters, and boat docks and ramps. The park hosts a gospel-music festival in April and a rare-birds event in October.

Continue south on GA 177. After 4.8 miles, you will reach a junction with U.S. 1; stay on GA 177 for 5.1 miles to Okefenokee Swamp Park. Along this route, you will travel through a corridor carved from a forest of thick pines. If you look carefully, you may see containers for catching resin attached to some of the trees.

*Entrance to
Okefenokee Swamp Park*

Okefenokee Swamp Park is a convenient point of entry and a magnificent showcase for the natural wonderland of the swamp. This scenic, nonprofit park has been the setting for a number of movies, among them *Swamp Water*, *Lure of the Wilderness*, and *Swamp Girl*. It offers canoeing, wildlife lectures, interpretive exhibits, and nature trails, all related to the half-million acres that comprise the Land of the Trembling Earth. If you happen to arrive at mealtime,

you may even get to see a park attendant feeding some of the many alligators. The cry of "Gatey! Gatey!" is all the invitation those fearsome animals need to come out of the water.

Be sure to take a guided tour of the swamp aboard one of the flat-bottomed boats that leave the dock at thirty-minute intervals. This not-to-be-missed excursion will take you through a foreign landscape of islands, lakes, jungles, forests, prairies, and lily-decked water trails. Among the sights you may see are 1,500-year-old cypresses, an old moonshine still, and an ancient Indian dugout canoe back in the trees. The boats glide past, over, and around more alligators than you can count; once you know what to look for, they are easy to spot, though they lie with only their eyes and a portion of their heads above the water. The black water of the Okefenokee is actually quite pure. It is also miraculously reflective. A favorite spot on the boat tour is Mirror Lake. The words on the sign for Mirror Lake are printed backwards, so that you have to look at their reflection in the lake to read them correctly.

When you are ready to leave Okefenokee Swamp Park, backtrack on GA 177 to U.S. 1 and turn right, heading south. Along this road, signs proclaiming "Trees Grow Jobs" will let you know that the timber business is alive and well in the pine forests of southern Georgia. Follow U.S. 1 for 26.7 miles to the junction with GA 121 in Folkston. Turn right. Follow GA 121 for 7.9 miles through a rural area to the gate for the Okefenokee National Wildlife Refuge. Turn right and proceed 4.1 miles to the entrance. A fee is charged except for senior citizens.

The Okefenokee National Wildlife Refuge offers guided boat tours of the portion of the swamp around Folkston. Visitors can camp overnight and rent canoes and boats. Be sure to try what the sign at the entrance calls the "Swamp Island Wildlife Drive," a quiet, shady, winding road of breathtaking beauty that weaves around a multitude of lagoons. Along the route, you will pass the Chesser Island Homestead, an old island house that is open for touring. Among the other attractions at the refuge are hiking trails, a 50-foot observation tower, the 12-mile-long Suwannee Canal, and a 4,000-foot scenic boardwalk into the Okefenokee. Again, the alligators are plentiful, and shorebirds are everywhere.

Okefenokee National Wildlife Refuge

Leaving the refuge, backtrack to Folkston and turn right on Love Street. Proceed 0.2 mile and turn right on U.S. 1. Continue one block and turn left on Main Street. After one block, turn right on Third Street. Follow Third for one block, then turn left on GA 40. Follow GA 40 for 19 miles to downtown Kingsland.

Kingsland was once owned by King George II. Some fifty-three years after Georgia was granted its charter, a man named John King acquired a large tract of land in the southeastern part of the state, becoming the largest landowner in what is now Camden County. His great-grandson, William Henry King, was the founder of Kingsland.

From the downtown intersection of GA 40 and U.S. 17, it is 4.3 miles on GA 40 to a sign for Base Road. Turn left. A drive of 3 miles will take you to the entrance to the Naval Submarine Base at King's Bay. This is the navy's East Coast base for Trident submarines, the strategic deterrent arm of our nation's submarine force. Visitors are not allowed.

Turn left at the base gate onto GA 40 Spur. It is a very short distance to the ruins of the tabby sugar works of John Houston McIntosh. The structure that once stood on this site was built around 1825 to process the sugar cane grown on McIntosh's Camden County plantation, New Canaan. It was said to house the first horizontal mill powered by cattle.

Sugar-works ruins on New Canaan Plantation

After McIntosh's death in 1836, New Canaan was sold to a Colonel Hallowes, who changed the name of the plantation to Bollingbrook. During the Civil War, Hallowes planted cane and made sugar in McIntosh's sugar works. He also used the structure as a starch factory, producing arrowroot starch in large quantities.

These tabby walls are among the oldest industrial ruins in Georgia.

When you are ready to leave the ruins, turn left on GA 40 Spur. It is 3.4 miles to Crooked River State Park; the substantial fence you will notice to the right during this drive encloses a portion of the submarine base.

The first thing you will notice about Crooked River State Park is how tropical it is. Florida is close by, and the landscape at the park will remind you of that of the Sunshine State. Among the amenities at the park are hiking trails, nature trails, miniature golf, an Olympic-size swimming pool, and eleven cottages overlooking the Crooked River.

Retrace your route to the sugar works, then continue on GA 40 Spur another 2.7 miles to the junction with GA 40. Turn left to visit the charming coastal village of St. Marys. Entering town, GA 40 becomes Osborne Street, the main street in St. Marys. It is 2.8 miles on GA 40/Osborne Street to the town's historic district, then another 0.4 mile to where Osborne ends at St. Marys Street and the river; the walking tour of St. Marys presented later in this tour covers the portion of Osborne Street divided by the median.

Turn right on St. Marys Street. On your left, you will see the National Park Service building, where you can make reservations for the boat trip to Cumberland Island included at the end of this tour. If you wish to take the boat trip, make plans to do so now; the earlier you request a reservation, the better your chance of getting a spot on the boat. The personnel at the ticket office can help you choose from among the available tours.

Inside the National Park Service building, you will notice a relief map of

Crooked River State Park

TOURING THE COASTAL GEORGIA BACKROADS

Cumberland Island that includes twelve braille markers outlining the island's highlights. St. Marys is the first city in Georgia to offer historical markers with raised letters and braille interpretations to aid the sight-impaired and the blind. Some thirty-eight such markers are scattered around the town.

Continue along St. Marys Street a short distance and leave your car in the parking lot on the right just before Bartlett Street. Retrace your route on foot along St. Marys Street to Osborne Street, where the walking tour of the historic district begins. This district was listed on the National Register of Historic Places in 1976.

In 1787, a man named Jacob Weed became the holder of a state grant for 1,620 acres on the north bank of the St. Marys River at a place called Buttermilk Bluff. Nineteen other men, among them Henry Osborne, who was a prominent circuit judge and a landowner in Brunswick, each paid Weed thirty-eight dollars for a share in the new settlement. That sum entitled them to four blocks of highland, certain marsh lots, and a share in the town commons. St. Marys was laid out by James Finley, the county surveyor, the following year. Today, the streets comprising the historic district are the same as those on the original town map.

Dr. Daniel Turner described the young town this way in an 1805 letter:

> The town of St. Marys is small—& appears to be agreeable of all. There are many respectable characters in it—the circle which I am making myself acquainted with is small, . . . [and] fashionable in form & appearance.
>
> The men in town are chiefly engaged in mercantile business—in Speculation. Cotton ginning, & steam mills—The planters generally both in Georgia and Florida are men of respectability, of information, & very hospitable. . . . What my business may be in 4 to 6 months, I can't know, but at present [I] feel very contented & tolerably well pleased— The country to be sure has no pleasant look to a stranger—but it is very productive.

Captain Morse House

Walk down the right side of Osborne Street. As you begin, you will notice a cannon from an old Spanish vessel gracing the median to your left.

The first long block stretching away from the river is taken up by commercial establishments. The most noteworthy among them are the last two buildings before Bryant Street. The Captain Morse House, built around 1905, is the yellow house with double porches and white trim at 124 Osborne. Formerly a private home, a boardinghouse, and a law office by turns, it now houses an

The Bachlott-Porter House

antique shop and ladies' boutique. On the corner of Bryant Street at 126 Osborne is the Stotesbury Johnson House, built around 1821. This small cottage-type bungalow is now the home of Blue Goose Country Collectibles.

Cross Bryant Street. The first home on your right is the Spencer House, built around 1872. This large clapboard house with double front porches operates as an inn today. The Bachlott-Porter House, the last house before Weed Street, has a gazebo back in the trees. Constructed in 1911 at a cost of $4,500, it now serves as a bed-and-breakfast inn.

Cross Weed Street. The home with double porches, white banisters, and a white picket fence you will see in the middle of the block is the John Rudulph House, constructed before 1879. Note that this home was built in the shape of a cross. All of its rooms have three-way exposure.

The last house before Conyers Street is the Jackson-Clark-Bessent-MacDonell House, dating from around 1801. This was once the home of Major Archibald Clark, a native of Savannah. After attending law school in Connecticut, Clark began practicing law here. President Thomas Jefferson later appointed him collector of the port of St. Marys, a position he held under nine presidents, serving until his death in 1848. In 1804, after his famous duel with Alexander Hamilton, Aaron Burr took refuge at Pierce Butler's plantation on St. Simons Island. While there, he came by boat to visit Clark at St. Marys. (For more about Aaron Burr's stay in Georgia, see The Marshes of Glynn Tour, pages 139–40.) Another prominent friend of Clark's, General Winfield Scott, also visited this house.

Turn right on Conyers Street. On your left, you will see the white frame St. Marys Methodist Chapel. This chapel was organized in 1799, when George Clark was sent as a missionary to this Georgia frontier town. The current building dates from 1858. When St. Marys was occupied by Federal troops during the Civil War, this chapel served as a quartermaster's depot and the place where animals were butchered.

Return to Osborne Street and turn right. The St. Marys Police Station occupies the first building in this block. Next to it, you will see a glass building with a tin roof. This building houses what is popularly known as the "Toonerville Trolley." Hand-built by Philip M. Hopper in 1928, this quaint vehicle rode the rails carrying passengers between St. Marys and Kingsland. Its moment in the national spotlight came when cartoonist Roy Crane featured it in his syndicated strip, "Wash Tubbs and Easy." In the 1970s, the Toonerville Trolley was briefly brought out of retirement and adapted for street use.

When you have enjoyed the trolley, cross to the opposite side of Osborne

Street to visit First Presbyterian Church. Dating from 1808, this high-off-the-ground church is the third-oldest church in Georgia, trailing only Jerusalem Lutheran Church at Ebenezer and Midway Congregational Church in Liberty County. Built as a community church and originally known as Independent Presbyterian Church, it was paid for by public subscription.

First Presbyterian Church figures prominently in local legend. Back in the days when St. Marys was a thriving port, efforts were made to smuggle goods through the port to avoid the payment of duty. On one occasion, in order to divert attention, a smuggler appropriated the minister's horse from the stable, led it up the steep steps of the church, and tied the bell rope around its neck. As might be expected, the frightened horse bobbed its head in an effort to free itself, and hearing the frantic ringing of the bell, the townspeople ran to the church. Another version of the tale says that the horse was actually hoisted into the belfry, and that it was the poor creature's neighing that brought people running. In either case, the smugglers were free to bring their goods ashore unmolested during the turmoil.

Visitors are welcome inside the sanctuary. The burial ground at the back of the building is visible from the windows.

Cross Conyers Street and head briefly to the median to enjoy an interesting bit of local history. On the day when George Washington was laid to rest at Mount Vernon, local services were held in his honor throughout the nation. The citizens of St. Marys walked to the town dock to meet a boat bearing a symbolic, flag-draped casket. The casket was carried up Osborne Street and buried in the median with due ceremony and the firing of guns. Six oak trees were planted to mark the spot; they have since been known as the "Washington Oaks." Only the stump of one of them remains today. A well driven on the site that same year has come to be known as the "Washington Pump."

From the median, head back across Osborne Street to see Orange Hall, located at the southwest corner of Osborne and Conyers.

First Presbyterian Church

This house was built in the 1820s by John and Laila Wood for their daughter and her husband, the Reverend Horace Pratt, the inaugural minister of First Presbyterian Church. The Woods and their daughter are buried on the grounds of the church.

The doors, windows, fluted columns, and Doric capitals of Orange Hall are considered perfect examples of Greek Revival architecture. The high-ceilinged rooms are decorated with period furniture, and large mirrors hang on the walls. Carved above a fireplace is this verse:

Happy is the home that shelters a friend.
O turn thy rudder thitherward awhile,
Here may the storm-beat vessel safely ryde!
This is the port of rest from troublous toyle,
The World's sweet Inn from pain and wearisome turmoyle.

Orange Hall

Today, Orange Hall houses the St. Marys Welcome Center, which offers museum house tours of the town.

Continue toward the river on Osborne Street. The first building across Weed Street is Sterling's Grocery. Merchant D. C. Sterling opened for business in St. Marys in 1869 with a total store stock valued at $1,600. The present building dates from 1896. Tom Sterling took over the business after his father's death in 1942.

Next to Sterling's Grocery is the Bacon-Burns House, a beige clapboard home with end chimneys. This house was built around 1830 by Dr. Henry Bacon. If you are familiar with the design of the famous "Charleston single house," the Bacon-Burns House may look familiar; it has two rooms downstairs and another two upstairs. The original kitchen was housed in a separate building.

The next building is the Rudulph-Riggins House, at 211 Osborne. Constructed around 1911, this white frame structure cost its builder, Howard Rudulph, only $2,500. It continues in use as a private home today.

Sandiford-Goodbread House

Next to the Rudulph-Riggins House at 209 Osborne is the Sandiford-Goodbread House, now known as the Goodbread Inn, a bed-and-breakfast establishment. Constructed around 1885, this home has upper and lower porches, with filigree on the columns of the lower porch. It came into the possession of Walter Goodbread, captain of the steamboat *Hildegarde*, in 1901.

The red-painted brick building on the corner of Bryant Street is the former home of the Bank of St. Marys, constructed around 1837. The bank moved to Columbus in 1843, after which the Louis Dufour family purchased the structure for use as a Catholic church. The interior is visible from the windows on the street.

The gray-painted brick building with red trim and awnings in the middle of the next block is the former home of the Bank of Camden County, which opened in 1911 and remained in operation until the 1930s. The building subsequently housed the Bank of Darien, People's Bank, and First South Bank. It is now an office building.

Cross Stable Alley. The Riverview Hotel, a flat-roofed building with double porches facing Osborne, is located at the corner of Osborne and St. Marys streets. This hotel was constructed in 1916 by a corporation whose principal owner was Katherine Wadley. Sally Brandon bought the property in 1931, and it is still controlled by members of her family today. It is interesting to stand on the double porches and try to imagine the busy harbor scene in the early part of the century, when the shipping trade catered not to tourists but to timber and cotton interests. Over the years, the Riverview has hosted such distinguished guests as author Marjorie Kinnan Rawlings, cartoonist Roy Crane, and Admiral Chester Nimitz.

Cumberland Queen *awaiting the boarding of passengers*

This ends the walking tour of St. Marys. If you intend to visit Cumberland Island, turn right on St. Marys Street and walk to where the *Cumberland Queen* is berthed. The land you see across the water is not Cumberland Island but Fernandina Beach, Florida. This portion of the St. Marys River has been a popular spot for boating activities since 1836, when a group of coastal residents organized the Aquatic Club of Georgia. That year, the club held races at St. Marys, with a prize of fifty dollars going to the winning boat. (For more information about the Aquatic Club, see The Marshes of Glynn Tour, page 128.)

Tours of Cumberland Island are quite popular among travelers in coastal Georgia. Visitors are advised to bring food, drinks, suntan lotion, insect repellant, comfortable shoes, rain gear, film, and sunglasses. Refreshments and souvenirs are sold on the ferry during the forty-five-minute cruise, but there are no stores on the island itself.

For many people, Cumberland Island is the quintessential Golden Isle. It is the largest of the nine major barrier islands that buffer the Georgia mainland from the open sea. It stretches approximately 16 miles along the state's southernmost shore and is about 3 miles wide at its broadest point.

The earliest name applied to the island was Missoe, an Indian word for sassafras. During the sixteenth and seventeenth centuries, zealous churchmen from Spain planted the banner of their king on the island and organized a mission under Father Baltasar Lopez. These Spanish Franciscans called the island San Pedro.

The debate between England and Spain over the ownership of the island began in the first half of the eighteenth century. Having established a settlement at Savannah and begun preparations for a town and fort at Frederica on St. Simons Island, James Oglethorpe realized it was only a matter of time before he would move south. He subsequently built two forts on Cumberland: Fort St. Andrews on the north end and Fort William on the south end.

The island was first called Cumberland in 1734. That year, Oglethorpe made a return trip to England and brought Tomo-chi-chi, the chief of the Yamacraw Indians, with him; Tomo-chi-chi had proven of great service in helping Oglethorpe's colonists establish themselves in Georgia. (For more information about Tomo-chi-chi, see The Lincoln's Christmas Gift Tour, pages 23–25.) One of the Indians who accompanied the great chief across the ocean was Toonahowi, his nephew, who was about thirteen at the time. Toonahowi quickly struck up a friendship with a British boy about his own age, William Augustus, the duke of Cumberland. They were supposedly quite a pair, one the dark-haired son of Indian royalty and the other the fair-haired son of the king of a major empire. When it was time for the Indians to return to America, Prince William presented Toonahowi with a gold watch, which soon became his most valued possession. Toonahowi subsequently requested that the island called San Pedro be renamed Cumberland in honor of his friend.

Much of the history of Cumberland Island is centered around Dungeness, located at the south end. The original Dungeness was a hunting lodge that James Oglethorpe constructed near Fort William. Oglethorpe supposedly chose the name in honor of the county seat of the County of Kent, England.

In the early 1780s, in gratitude for services rendered, the people of Georgia gave Revolutionary War hero Nathanael Greene the deed to Mulberry Grove Plantation, located near Savannah. Greene soon began buying small parcels on Cumberland, and it wasn't long before he amassed considerable landholdings there. He was in the process of drawing up plans for a mansion and extensive gardens on Cumberland when he died in 1786. (For more information about Nathanael Greene, see The Lincoln's Christmas Gift Tour, pages 21–22.)

His wife, Catherine, continued his work. Located near the site of Oglethorpe's hunting lodge, the new mansion was also called Dungeness. It was a stupendous undertaking. The tabby walls of the four-story Dungeness were six feet thick at the base. The mansion contained sixteen fireplaces, which fed into four chimneys. A high masonry wall was constructed to encircle some twelve acres, which were to be devoted to the cultivation of flowers and tropical fruit. The home was not "completed" until 1803. Even then, according to a superstition of the Greene family, some of the rooms of Dungeness were left unfinished, as it was believed that misfortune would befall a completed home.

Some years after Nathanael Greene's death, Catherine married Phineas Miller, the longtime tutor of the Greene children. Another family tutor attained lasting fame—Eli Whitney, inventor of the cotton gin. Whitney did much of his work on the invention at Mulberry Grove, but he supposedly put the finishing touch on it during a trip to Dungeness—and gave Catherine the credit for inspiring him. As the story goes, the frustrated Whitney was demonstrating a model of the gin but was dissatisfied with the results. Catherine, one of the observers, supposedly announced, "Why, Mr. Whitney, you want a brush," then took her handkerchief and wiped away the lint that was hampering the machine's operation. Whitney adopted the idea and subsequently completed his great invention.

Phineas Miller came to a bad end in 1806 while trying to make improvements to the Dungeness property. He was removing orange trees from Florida for replanting on Cumberland when he inadvertently stuck an orange thorn through his hand; he later died of lockjaw.

During the War of 1812, United States troops were stationed at St. Marys. Formerly the wife of a man who had won lasting fame fighting the British, Catherine Greene Miller was delighted to see the two countries at war again. She entertained the officers stationed at St. Marys with dinner parties at Dungeness. Catherine died in 1814. The Dungeness property passed to her daughter, a Mrs. Louisa Catherine Shaw.

Early in 1818, a schooner cast anchor off Cumberland Island and an old gentleman, weak and suffering, came ashore. He introduced himself as Light Horse Harry Lee and explained that he had come to die in the arms of Mrs. Shaw, the daughter of his old friend and compatriot Nathanael Greene. Mrs. Shaw welcomed Lee and tried to make him comfortable during his last days. Though he remained under the close care of military surgeons throughout his stay, the old general died on March 25. He was laid to rest in the cemetery at Dungeness. During his funeral service, a small fleet of naval vessels in Cumberland Sound flew their flags at half-mast and fired a salute in his honor.

Robert E. Lee sent a tombstone to mark his father's resting place, and it is believed that he also visited the grave at Dungeness before, during, and after the Civil War. The remains of Light Horse Harry Lee were later removed from Cumberland Island and reinterred in Lexington, Virginia, next to those of his famous son.

Dungeness was stripped and looted by Union forces during the Civil War, then burned during Reconstruction. The family never returned.

In 1882, most of Cumberland Island was bought by Thomas Carnegie, the younger brother of financier Andrew Carnegie. Thomas Carnegie pulled down the ruins of the previous Dungeness and prepared to erect a new mansion on the old foundation, but like Nathanael Greene before him, he died before the project was completed. And like Catherine Greene before her, Lucy

Coleman Carnegie finished the project in grand style. The new mansion, too, was called Dungeness, and it was under Lucy Carnegie that this property gained its widest fame. Lucy was the first female member of the prestigious New York Yacht Club, and she subsequently named her yacht the *Dungeness*. A piece of music, the "Waltz Dungeness," was also composed in honor of the home on Cumberland Island. Guests of the Carnegies enjoyed polo, fencing, croquet, fishing, and hunting, along with swimming in the ocean or a heated pool. One famous hole on the Dungeness golf course measured only sixty yards, but it was equipped with so many hazards that golfers considered themselves lucky to complete it in only three or four strokes.

Dungeness was remodeled several times before it was finally left uninhabited in the 1950s. It burned in 1959.

Developers became interested in Cumberland in the 1960s, and the island was in danger of commercialization until Cumberland Island National Seashore was established in 1972. Today, the island is considered one of the most outstanding seashore areas in the country.

Visitors to Cumberland are rarely disappointed in what they find. If you disembark at Dungeness, make sure you visit the museum housed in the Carnegie icehouse, located near the dock. Only by seeing old photographs and documents relating to the Carnegies can you fully comprehend the grandeur of the island around the turn of the century.

Cumberland Island Museum

Dungeness ruins

When you have visited the museum, follow the trail to the Dungeness ruins. Even after seeing old photographs of the mansion in its heyday, you will be surprised at the grand scale of the ruins, where stairways, towers, and walls reach toward the sky.

Other structures and ruins are nearby. The Tabby House, located near the Dungeness ruins, is the oldest home on Cumberland Island. This structure, dating from around 1800, was used as the gardener's house in the days when Catherine Greene ran the estate. Though the Carnegie family subsequently pulled down the remains of Dungeness, they spared this two-story tabby structure. Lucy Carnegie later converted it for use as an office for year-round management of the estate.

Continue on the trail from the ruins to the ocean. You will pass the collapsed recreation house, the old stables, and the cemetery, which contains the remains of Catherine Greene Miller, Phineas Miller, and Mr. and Mrs. Shaw, among others.

The last portion of the trail passes through sand dunes. Two dune systems have developed here. The primary dunes border the beach, while the larger rear dunes provide protection from storms. The beach itself is pristine, cluttered only by nearly every variety of seashell common to the Southeast. A walk on the beach is a must. Visitors usually walk to Sea Camp and then make a complete circle by heading back through the woods to the Dungeness dock.

Dungeness is the most popular stop on Cumberland, but it is actually only the southern tip of an island that holds many more attractions for those who are willing to explore. Several mansions remain, most of them built by the Carnegies when the island was divided among the family members. Grand Avenue, once an active road running the length of the island, is today no more than a two-track lane bordered by thick vegetation. A few paths lead from Grand Avenue to the remaining estates, some of which are privately owned and others of which are controlled by the National Park Service. North of Dungeness is Greyfield, now operated as an exclusive hotel. Farther north is the mansion called Stafford, then Plum Orchard, which is operated as a museum. At the far north end of the island is High Point.

Visitors to Cumberland can count on meeting some of the island's wild inhabitants, which include deer, turkeys, horses, armadillos, squirrels, rabbits, and otters—and even alligators and snakes. If you're lucky, you may get to see wild horses nibbling grass among the ruins of a great mansion. It is an experience you will not soon forget.

This tour ends on Cumberland Island.

Wild horses roam the Dungeness ruins

The Tabby House

Appendix

Federal Agencies

Cumberland Island
National Seashore
National Park Service
P.O. Box 806
St. Marys, GA 31558
912-882-4335 (for reservations)
912-882-4336 (for information)

Fort Frederica National
Monument National Park Service
Route 9, Box 286-C
St. Simons Island, GA 31522
912-638-3639

Fort Pulaski National Monument
National Park Service
P.O. Box 98
Tybee Island, GA 31328
912-786-5787

Museum of Coastal History
P.O. Box 1136
St. Simons Island, GA 31522

Okefenokee National Wildlife
Refuge
U.S. Fish & Wildlife Service
Route 2, Box 338
Folkston, GA 31537
912-496-7836

St. Simons Lighthouse
U.S. Coast Guard
101 12th Street
St. Simons Island, GA 31522
912-638-4666

State Parks and Agencies

Crooked River State Park
Georgia Department of
Natural Resources
3092 Spur 40
St. Marys, GA 31558
912-882-5256

Fort King George
Georgia Department of
Natural Resources
P.O. Box 711
Darien, GA 31305
912-437-4770

Fort McAllister
Georgia Department of
Natural Resources
Richmond Hill State Park
Route 2, Box 394-A
Richmond Hill, GA 31324
912-727-2339

Fort Morris Historic Site
Georgia Department of Natural
Resources
Route 1, Box 236
Midway, GA 31320
912-884-5999

Georgia Tourism Council
P.O. Box 1291
St. Marys, GA 31558
912-882-4000
912-882-6200

Hofwyl-Broadfield Plantation
Georgia Department of
Natural Resources
Route 10, Box 83
Brunswick, GA 31520
912-264-9263

Jekyll Island Museum
Georgia Department of
Natural Resources
375 Riverview Drive
Jekyll Island, GA 31527
912-635-2119

Laura S. Walker State Park
Georgia Department of
Natural Resources
Route 6, Box 205
Waycross, GA 31501
912-283-4424

McIntosh County Welcome
Center Georgia Department of
Natural Resources
P.O. Box 1497
Darien, GA 31305
912-437-6684

Skidaway Institute
of Oceanography
University of Georgia
P.O. Box 13687
Savannah, GA 31416
912-598-2496

Skidaway Island State Park
Georgia Department of
Natural Resources
52 Diamond Causeway
Savannah, GA 31411
912-598-2300

Wormsloe State Historic Site
Georgia Department of
Natural Resources
7601 Skidaway Road
Savannah, GA 31406
912-352-2548

County Parks and Agencies

**Brunswick/Golden Isles
Visitors Bureau**
4 Glynn Avenue
Brunswick, GA 31520
800-933-COAST

**Darien Welcome Center/McIntosh
County Chamber of Commerce**
P.O. Box 1497
Darien, GA 31305
912-437-4192

**Folkston/Charlton County
Chamber of Commerce**
P.O. Box 756
Folkston, GA 31537
912-496-2536

**Fort Jackson
Coastal Heritage Society**
1 Fort Jackson Road
Savannah, GA 31404
912-232-3945

**Hinesville/Liberty County
Chamber of Commerce**
P.O. Box 405
Hinesville, GA 31313
912-368-4445

Kingsland Tour and Travel
P.O. Box 1928
Kingsland, GA 31548
912-729-5999

**Richmond Hill Chamber
of Commerce**
P.O. Box 1067
Richmond Hill, GA 31324
912-756-2676

**St. Simons Island Chamber
of Commerce and Visitors Center**
530-B Beachview Drive
St. Simons Island, GA 31522
912-638-9014

Savannah History Museum
303 Martin Luther King, Jr.,
Boulevard
Savannah, GA 31401
912-238-1779

Savannah Visitors Center
301 Martin Luther King, Jr.,
Boulevard
Savannah, GA 31401
912-944-0456

**Tybee Island
Chamber of Commerce**
209 Butler Avenue
Tybee Island, GA 31328
912-786-5444

**Waycross/Ware County Tourist
and Convention Bureau**
P.O. Box 137
Waycross, GA 31501
912-283-3742

Others

Bethesda Home for Boys
P.O. Box 13039
Savannah, GA 31416

Bonaventure Cemetery
330 Bonaventure Road
Savannah, GA 31404
912-235-4227

Claxton Bakery, Inc.
P.O. Box 367
Claxton, GA 30417
912-739-3441

**Epworth-by-the-Sea
South Georgia Methodist
Conference**
P.O. Box 407
St. Simons Island, GA 31522
912-638-8688

**Goodbread House Bed and
Breakfast**
209 Osborne Street
St. Marys, GA 31558
912-882-7490

Isaiah Davenport House Museum
324 East State Street
Savannah, GA 31401
912-236-8097

**John H. Swisher and Son, Inc.,
Cigar Manufacturers**
P.O. Box 137
Waycross, GA 31501
912-283-3742

Juliette Gordon Low Center
142 Bull Street
Savannah, GA 31401
912-233-4501

**Little St. Simons Island
Information**
P.O. Box 1078RC
St. Simons Island, GA 31522

**Methodist Museum
South Georgia Methodist
Conference**
P.O. Box 407
St. Simons Island, GA 31522
912-638-4050

Midway Museum
P.O. Box 195
Midway, GA 31320

Museum of Coastal History
P.O. Box 21136
101 12th Street
St. Simons Island, GA 31522
912-638-4666

**New Ebenezer Family Retreat
and Conference Center**
Route 1, Box 478
Rincon, GA 31326
912-754-9142

Obediah's Okefenok
P.O. Box 423
Waycross, GA 31502
912-287-0090

Okefenokee Heritage Center
Box 406B
Waycross, GA 31501
912-285-4260
912-285-4058

Okefenokee Swamp Park
Waycross, GA 31501
912-283-0583

Orange Hall/
St. Marys Welcome Center
P.O. Box 1291
St. Mary's, Georgia 31558
912-882-4000

Owens-Thomas House
and Museum
124 Abercorn Street
Savannah, GA 31401
912-233-9734

Pirates' House Restaurant
East Broad and Bay streets
Savannah, GA 31401
912-233-5757

Riverview Hotel
105 Osborne Street
St. Marys, GA 31558
912-882-3242

Savannah Science Museum
4405 Paulsen Street
Savannah, GA 31401
912-355-6705

Ships of the Sea Maritime Mu-
seum
503 East River Street/504 East Bay
Street
Savannah, GA 31401
912-232-1511

Southern Forest World
Route 5, Box 406A
Waycross, GA 31501
912-285-4260
912-285-4058

Spencer House Inn
101 East Bryant Street
St. Marys, GA 31558
912-882-1872

Telfair Mansion and Art Museum
121 Barnard Street
Savannah, GA 31401
912-233-9743

Tybee Island Museum
and Lighthouse
P.O. Box 366
Tybee Island, GA 31328
912-786-5801

Selected Bibliography

Blassingame, John W., ed. *Slave Testimony: Two Centuries of Letters, Speeches, Interviews, and Autobiographies*. Baton Rouge: Louisiana State University Press, 1977.

Bragg, Lillian C. *Stories of Old Savannah*. Second Series, 1949.

Colquitt, Harriet Ross. *The Savannah Cook Book*. New York: Farrar & Rinehart, 1933.

Conniff, Richard. "Blackwater Country." *National Geographic* 181, no. 4 (April 1992): 34–63.

Gamble, Thomas. *Savannah Duels and Duellists, 1733–1877*. Spartanburg, S.C.: The Reprint Company, 1974.

Georgia Salzburger Society. *Ye Olde Time Salzburger Cook Book*. 1925.

Georgia Writers' Project. *Drums and Shadows*. Athens and London: University of Georgia Press, 1986.

Godley, Margaret. *Historic Tybee Island*. Savannah Beach Chamber of Commerce, 1958.

———. *Stories of Old Savannah*. Second Series, 1949.

Harden, William. *A History of Savannah and South Georgia*. Vol. 1. 1913.

Johnson, Amanda. *Georgia As Colony and State*. Atlanta: Walter Brown Publishing, 1938.

Jones, Charles C., Jr. *History of Savannah, Ga*. Syracuse, N.Y.: D. Mason & Company, 1890.

Joyner, Charles. *Remember Me: Slave Life in Coastal Georgia*. Atlanta: Georgia Humanities Council, Georgia History and Culture Series, 1989.

Kemble, Frances Anne. *Journal of a Residence on a Georgian Plantation, 1838–39*. Edited and with an introduction by John A. Scott. New York: Alfred A. Knopf, 1961.

Knight, L. L. *Georgia Landmarks, Memorials and Legends*. Vol. 2. Atlanta: Bird Printing Company, 1914.

Knight, Lucian Lamar. *Georgia's Bi-centennial Memoirs and Memories*. By the author, 1933.

McAllister, Samuel Ward. *Society As I Have Found It*. New York: Arno Press, 1975.

McKee, Gwen, ed. *A Guide of the Georgia Coast*. Savannah: The Georgia Conservancy, 1988.

Miller, Mary. *Cumberland Island, The Unsung Northend*. Darien: The Darien News, 1990.

Rogers, George C., Jr. *The History of Georgetown County, South Carolina*. Columbia: University of South Carolina Press, 1970.

Savannah Unit of the Federal Writers' Project. *Savannah River Plantations*. Works Progress Administration of Georgia.

Sieg, Chan. *The Squares: An Introduction to Savannah*. Norfolk, Va.: The Donning Company, 1984.

Sojourn in Savannah: An Official Guidebook and Map of Savannah and the Surrounding Countryside. Savannah: 1990.

Thomas, David Hurst. *St. Catherines: An Island in Time*. Georgia Endowment for the Humanities, Georgia History and Culture Series, 1988.

Vanstory, Burnette. *Georgia's Land of the Golden Isles*. Athens: University of Georgia Press, 1981.

Wilson, Adelaide. *Historic and Picturesque Savannah*. Boston: The Boston Photogravure Company, 1889.

Young, Claiborne. *Cruising Guide to Coastal South Carolina and Georgia*. Winston-Salem, N.C.: John F. Blair, Publisher, 1993.

Index